CHOC

Other titles in the series:

Shaping the Tools: Study Skills in Theology
by Ruth Ackroyd and David Major

God's World by Jeff Astley

Using the Bible: Studying the Text by Robert Evans

Literature in Christian Perspective: Becoming Faithful Readers
by Bridget Nichols

Being Anglican by Alastair Redfern

Ministry and Priesthood by Alastair Redfern

*God's Here and Now: Social Contexts of the Ministry of the People of
God* by Philip Richter

The Authority of the Bible by William Strange

Living Theology by Michael West, Graham Noble and Andrew Todd

SERIES EDITORS: Leslie J Francis and Jeff Astley

CHOOSING LIFE?

Christianity and Moral Problems

Jeff Astley

DARTON·LONGMAN+TODD

First published in 2000 by
Darton, Longman and Todd Ltd
1 Spencer Court
140-142 Wandsworth High Street
London SW18 4JJ

ISBN 0-232-52368-1

Designed by Sandie Boccacci
Phototypeset in Minion by Intype London Ltd
Printed and bound in Great Britain by
Page Bros, Norwich, Norfolk

CONTENTS

Acknowledgements   vi

Preface   vii

Introduction   ix

1. The good, the bad and the righteous?   1

2. Morality in debate   12

3. Christian resources   24

4. What is a life worth?   38

5. Sex and society   49

6. Wealth and work   61

7. War and punishment   73

8. Disagreeing with our neighbours   86

9. Teaching right from wrong   98

10. Religion and moral choice   109

References   119

Glossary and biography   126

Index of themes   129

Applying for the Church Colleges' Certificate Programme   133

ACKNOWLEDGEMENTS

Quotations from the Bible are from the *New Revised Standard Version* Bible, © 1989, by the Division of Christian Education of the National Council of the Churches of Christ in the USA, and are used by permission. All rights reserved.

I am grateful to the editors and publishers of the *International Journal of Education and Religion* for permission to use material first published in this journal.

PREFACE

At the beginning of the third millennium a new mood is sweeping through the Christian Churches. This mood is reflected in a more radical commitment to discipleship among a laity who wish to be theologically informed and fully equipped for Christian ministry in the secular world.

Exploring Faith: theology for life is designed for people who want to take Christian theology seriously. Taken seriously, Christian theology engages the mind, involves the heart, and seeks active expression in the way we live. Those who explore their faith in this way are beginning to shape a theology for life.

Exploring Faith: theology for life is rooted in the individual experience of the world and in the ways through which God is made known in the world. Such experience is related to and interpreted in the light of the Christian tradition. Each volume in the series takes a key aspect of theology, and explores this aspect in dialogue with the readers' own experience. Each volume is written by a scholar who has clear authority in the area of theology discussed and who takes seriously the ways in which busy adults learn.

The volumes are suitable for all those who wish to learn more about the Christian faith and ministry, including those who have already taken Christian basic courses (such as *Alpha* and *Emmaus*) and have been inspired to undertake further study, those preparing to take theology as an undergraduate course, and those already engaged on degree programmes. The volumes have been developed for individuals to work on alone or for groups to study together.

Already groups of Christians are using the *Exploring Faith: theology for life* series throughout the United Kingdom, linked by an exciting initiative pioneered jointly by the Anglican dioceses, the Board of Education of the Church and World Division and the Ministry Division of the Archbishops' Council of the Church of England, the National Society and the Church Colleges. Used in this way each volume can earn credits towards one of the Church Colleges' Certificates and provide access to degree level study. Further information about the Church Colleges' Certificate Programme is provided on page 133.

The Church Colleges' Certificate Programme integrates well with the lifelong learning agenda which now plays such a crucial role in educational priorities. Learning Christians can find their way into degree-bearing programmes through this series *Exploring Faith: theology for life* linked with the Church Colleges' Certificates.

This series of books originated in materials developed by and for the Aston Training Scheme. Thanks are due to former staff of the Scheme, and in particular to Roger Spiller who conceived of and commissioned the original series, and to Nicola Slee who edited the original materials. In the light of the closure of Aston, this series represents something of the ongoing contribution of the Scheme to the life of the Church.

In preparing a series of this kind, much work is done behind the scenes. Financial and staff support have been generously given by the Ministry Division. Thanks are due to Marilyn Parry for the vision of bringing together the Aston materials and the Anglican Church Colleges of Higher Education. We are also grateful for financial support from the following Church Colleges: Chester College; Christchurch University College, Canterbury; The College of St Mark & St John, Plymouth; St Martin's College, Lancaster; Trinity College, Carmarthen and Whitelands College (Roehampton Institute). Without the industry, patience, perception, commitment and skill of Ruth Ackroyd this series would have remained but a dream.

The series editors wish to express their personal thanks to colleagues who have helped them shape the series identity, especially Diane Drayson, Evelyn Jackson and Katie Worrall, and to the individual authors who have produced high quality text on schedule and so generously accepted firm editorial direction. The editorial work has been supported by the North of England Institute for Christian Education and the Centre for Ministry Studies at the University of Wales, Bangor.

Leslie J Francis
Jeff Astley

INTRODUCTION

This book addresses basic issues about the character of morality and the choices facing people in a variety of moral situations. These concerns are not restricted to members of the Church or of any faith community. Being a Christian does not make these issues and choices any simpler and Christianity rarely provides a single answer to the moral dilemma, 'What should I do now?'

That question, relentlessly pursued, can lead us to do some very hard thinking indeed. Moral reflection, including reflection on the very nature of morality, will engage us in the most demanding sort of intellectual effort, where clear answers are difficult to find. Unlike many other kinds of thinking, however, moral reflection is often demanded of us because we *have* to decide. We have to *do* something, to make some choices, despite the difficulties we face in resolving the moral puzzle that is before us.

Readers should not come to this book expecting easy answers, then. Ethics is not like that. Besides which, we all have to decide for ourselves when faced by moral dilemmas. Books, like other people, can help those decisions to be more informed and more reflective; but no one can do your moral thinking and decision-making for you.

That is true even of religious people. Those Christians who find moral decision-making unproblematic, because they have a clear sense of what a Christian morality should be, must still decide to adopt that morality for themselves (Nowell-Smith, 1999, p. 405). They should try to recognise that other, equally sincere, Christians may properly make a different decision based on a different understanding of Christian morality and of the identity and role of Christian 'moral authorities', or of the relevance of these things to any given moral problem.

Choosing Life? should prove useful for adult Christian learners and for introductory courses in ethics in sixth forms, colleges and universities. Much of the material in this book has its origins in courses that I have taught in all these different contexts.

1. THE GOOD, THE BAD AND THE RIGHTEOUS?

Introduction

We cannot avoid making choices. To be human, and especially to be an adult, is to be forced to make decisions. Many of these decisions are trivial: what to wear, what to have for lunch, who to invite to your party. But others seem much more serious, for they have a 'moral dimension'.

This book is about moral decision-making, particularly in a Christian context. Because we all make such decisions, it is very much about real life – our own and that of other people, especially at moments of crisis or of deep concern.

Reflecting on experience
Think back over the past seven days. From all the decisions you made in that period, and all the situations in which you found yourself, choose just two that you would describe as having a moral dimension. What was 'moral' about them?

According to the dictionaries, the adjective 'moral' means something like this: 'concerned with goodness or badness of character or disposition, or with the distinction between right and wrong'. Your reflections probably involved the use of this language of goodness/badness and right/wrong. Such language can be used quite generally. We speak of an apple being 'bad' or about the 'right' way of spelling a word, without implying any moral claim. But where a moral dimension is noted, this same language is used for a distinctively different sort of *moral evaluation*. Once we are in the moral realm, a characteristically moral vocabulary is available to us. We may speak of our 'duty' or 'obligation', of 'principles' and 'rights', of 'character' or 'virtue', of 'conscience' and 'motive', and even (if we are religious) of 'sin'.

Ethics and morality

Many writers take these two words as synonymous, except that ethics is also used as a label for the more theoretical, reflective and self-conscious study of morality (or 'moral philosophy'). There is a lot to be said for this approach, for those who distinguish morality and ethics do so in a number of different ways (for example sometimes ethics is seen as collective or societal, and morality as individual).

What should we do?

Let us look first at someone else's moral dilemma. It is one of many such stories in this book. Apart from the names, this is a true account.

Dilemma: the tanker crash

A young mother, Susan, was parked outside a nursery school when her vehicle was hit by a petrol tanker. The driver of the tanker, Gavin, immediately admitted liability and seemed eager to pay for the damage, 'as long as you don't tell my firm – I'm not supposed to be here'. However, on later hearing that the repairer's estimate came to several hundred pounds, Gavin suggested that Susan should put in a claim against his firm's insurance but tell them that the accident had happened in another street.

When Susan refused, Gavin said that he would probably lose his job if it were discovered that he had been off his route. He had a wife and a sick child to support, and a heavy mortgage. In any case, he continued, if Susan stuck to her story he would deny it all and then her claim would be contested and might even go to court. She surely would not want that.

EXERCISE
- What do you think that Susan ought to do, and why?
- What, if anything, is wrong with Gavin's proposal?

- Do you have any comments to make about the character of Gavin or Susan?
- Is there any religious dimension to this situation?

What moral language would you use here? You might be thinking that 'Susan is in the right' or that 'She hasn't done anything wrong.' You might be critical of (or 'blame') Gavin for his attitude and for encouraging her to tell a lie. On the other hand, you could think that Susan 'ought' to fall in with his request, considering the bad consequences that could result for Gavin and his family if she does tell the truth. Perhaps you would 'admire' Susan if she takes this line, for this reason; or perhaps you would only admire her if she shows 'integrity' and 'sticks to her principles' of not telling lies and refusing to be used.

What else might govern Susan's decision? Gavin appealed to what Susan might 'want'. Is that relevant? Is ethics about what we want or what we ought to do regardless of what we want?

The story might have struck you as a poor example of a *moral* dilemma. You might think differently about it if the situation were adjusted a little.

Dilemma: the second crash

In this case, Gavin hits someone else's vehicle and Susan is the only witness. He begins to drive off but Susan flags him down. Gavin proposes leaving £50 ('It's all I've got') under the windscreen wiper of the damaged car and asks Susan to keep quiet about it. The situation then continues as in the second paragraph of the earlier dilemma.

EXERCISE
Do these modifications change how you react to the situation? Are you more likely now to see Susan's dilemma as a *moral* dilemma and if so, why is this?

You may be more willing to use 'ought' language here, with regard to Susan's decision, because the story is now about how far she should be concerned for *other people* rather than a loss or injury that she has sustained herself.

Ought language is not just used of moral obligations, of course. 'You ought to wear your green top with that skirt' and 'You ought to move your queen' are non-moral obligations. They are examples of what the philosopher Immanuel Kant called 'hypothetical imperatives'. They are conditional on something else, usually something you want, spoken or unspoken: 'If you want to look good, you ought to wear your green top'; 'If you don't want it taken, you should move your queen.' But moral imperatives are unconditional (or 'categorical'). They cannot serve as an answer to a question of the form, 'What ought I to do, *if* I want . . . (my car repaired, to keep out of court or to ensure that Gavin likes me)?' These conditions relate to what we desire and will vary from person to person. Kant thought that they were irrelevant to morality.

Universal and impartial?

Another way of expressing this is to say that moral ought statements imply some sort of *universalisability*. This means that if Susan ought to do *x*, then anyone else in the same situation ought to do *x* also; and they ought to do it, as Susan ought, whether she wants to or not. Note that a universalisable principle is not necessarily a general, unspecific one, such as 'Always tell the truth' or 'Never let the innocent suffer.' It can be quite detailed and specific ('Always tell the truth, except when it may harm others to do so, and except when . . . etc.'). Susan's principle of action may be very specific: 'When faced with this sort of situation [as detailed in the first dilemma], I ought (or ought not) to report the driver.'

Moral ought judgements implicitly prescribe the same action to anyone in the same situation. So if it is right for Susan to do something, I ought to do it too if faced by her dilemma. If it is wrong for her, it would be wrong for me also, given the same situation. In applying a moral rule I cannot make an exception for myself, unless there is a good moral reason for my case to be treated differently.

While no two situations, and the responsibilities and powers of no two agents, are ever exactly alike, they are often *morally identical*. This means that in all particulars that are morally relevant, the two situations are just the same. Sometimes they are not: although *I* ought to jump in the river to save a child *you* may not have the same duty, perhaps because you cannot swim or because you have to hold on to two little children. But the fact that your hair is a different colour from mine, that your income is twice as great, or that you don't want to risk *your* life, is morally irrelevant.

What it means to say that an action is 'right', then, is this: an action is right if I ought to perform it (and wrong if I ought not to perform it) *and* if everyone else in a morally identical situation ought to perform it as well (or ought not to).

EXERCISE
Do you accept this? Are situations sufficiently alike (morally) to make this claim?

Another aspect of a true moral judgement is its *impartiality*. In the moral point of view, each person matters equally. Morality is impartial. The universalisability of moral judgements is a sort of impartiality: if this is right/wrong for me, it is right/wrong for everyone in the same situation. But impartiality may go deeper than this. It may mean that there is a *common point of view* in moral justification, so that in our second dilemma the owner of the car that was struck by Gavin's tanker matters just as much as does Gavin or Susan. Each person matters equally. This finds religious expression in claims such as 'We are all God's children.' It certainly means that the hurt or the rights of every other person involved must be given as high a status as I ascribe to my own hurt and rights.

But does that mean that I can never be partial in my actions?

Dilemma: the freak wave

Imagine that you are alone on a windswept pier, or on a boat in the middle of a lake, in charge of two toddlers. A sudden freak wave takes them both into the water. You can only save one of them because of limitations of time, strength or rescue equipment.

EXERCISE
Who would you try to save under these different circumstances:
- if one was your own child and the other unrelated;
- if both were unrelated to you, but one was very seriously mentally handicapped? ▶▶

What if you decide that it is right to prefer one child (say it is your daughter and that the other child is terminally ill) but you cannot hold on to her because the second child is clinging too tightly. Would you then be justified in pushing the second child out of the way, with the result that he drowned?

Active and passive morality

One of the confessions in *The Book of Common Prayer* speaks of our penitence both for doing 'those things which we ought not to have done' and for leaving undone 'those things which we ought to have done', that is for sins both of *commission* and of *omission*. This distinction, and the related one between doing something and just letting it happen, are of some significance in ethics.

Many people would say that it is a far more serious matter for us to act than for us to sit by and let Nature take its course (or, in some cases, let another person's actions take their course). We are, after all, responsible for our own actions but not for those of other people or of Nature (or of God?).

EXERCISE
Is there a moral difference between our positive actions and our inaction? Should I be blamed for something that I did not do but could have prevented? Can you think of examples of such situations?

Morally speaking, is it more important not to harm someone than it is to help them?

Although we may be said to have 'positive responsibility' for the acts that we perform, we often think that we ought to take some sort of responsibility ('negative responsibility') for those events that we could have prevented but did not, such as deaths from a famine, as well as for those events that were the *unintended* consequences of our intentional acts.

As we shall see in subsequent chapters, there is a strong Christian voice that would only permit abortion, euthanasia or other killings in those cases where this (evil) result happens as a side effect of some intervention that intends a good consequence: a life-saving operation for a pregnant woman or an injection of morphine for a terminally ill patient in great pain. Other moralists are critical of this *doctrine of double (or second) effect* (see Chapter 2).

In all of this, there is a contrast to be drawn between a morality that focuses on the agent, his intentions and moral purity, and one that focuses on people other than the agent, their needs and their welfare. Christian morality has sometimes been criticised for getting that focus wrong, through an overriding concern about the health of our soul. 'A Christian is supposed to lose his life, not to save it . . . We should forget about sin, guilt and self-conquest, and concentrate on being kind to each other instead: the results will be far better' (Cupitt, 1988, pp. 27, 56). What do you think?

Moral obligation and moral value

We may usefully distinguish between *our duty* and *what we value*. Judgements of moral value differ from judgements of moral obligation in the language they use: instead of speaking of right and wrong, and using ought language, they speak of what is good or bad. They answer the question 'What things are good (or worthwhile)?' rather than 'What things ought we to do?'

Theories of value distinguish two types of value:

• *extrinsic or instrumental value* is value that is to be found outside a thing, when it is valued for its effects ('instrumentally');
• *intrinsic value* is value that is found within something, when it is valued 'for itself' ('intrinsically') and regarded as 'good for its own sake'. (Note that nothing could have instrumental value unless some other things were valued in and of themselves.)

What things are of intrinsic value? Some have held that pleasure is the only intrinsic value; but most would argue that there are many values and perhaps that anything that is the object of positive interest for us (we are 'for' it) is a value. On another account, 'self-realisation' (fulfilling the purpose of our own existence) is the only intrinsic good.

We may ask, however, whether these are *moral* values. While it may seem fitting to concentrate on moral values such as a good character, some non-moral values do seem to have a place in what has been called *the good life*. Such a life may be characterised by such features as freedom, authenticity and fulfilment, or knowledge and reason, or harmony and contentment, as well as (or rather than?) kindness and integrity.

Sometimes the term 'ethics' is taken to label this wider category *of the life that is worth living*. Our moral obligations might be thought of as ultimately dependent on some sort of claim about what it is to be truly ourselves or truly human, which is a claim about what the authentically good life is like and what really constitutes human well-being or 'human flourishing'.

Many have argued that *moral virtue* is the only intrinsic good and that the good or flourishing life is simply the life lived in accordance with these virtues.

Doing and being

A great deal of recent writing in philosophical and Christian ethics has focused, as Aristotle did, on an ethic of virtue (MacIntyre, 1981; Hauerwas, 1981; Slote, 1997). This quest for virtue moves us beyond discussions of obligation to a focus on 'who we *are* (or ought to be) – rather than what we *do*'.

> Perhaps the ethical life is not primarily a function of the actions that people engage in but a function of the kind of people that engage in the actions. Maybe we should turn our focus away from action and become concerned with character and virtue, and only then speak about the actions that emerge from the virtuous person. In short, maybe we should abandon the search for an ethic of doing and seek instead to devise an ethic of *being* (or of virtue). (Grenz, 1997, pp. 39–40)

This view exalts character over conduct and places the emphasis on people's motives and character traits, especially such dispositions as their honesty, courage, caring, faithfulness and humility. These aspects of character seem to be good in themselves. 'The seemingly self-justifying character of the life of the saint' (Mackinnon, 1957, p. 59) might suggest this rather different view of ethics.

Living virtue

Of course, being and doing are related. We know a person's character through their actions (including their 'verbal actions', that is their words). My actions express my character, as my dispositions produce effects in the world or for myself that may be judged good or bad. So virtues give rise to good conduct: veracity disposes us to truth telling, fidelity to promise keeping. Further, conduct lays down character. Thus behaving humbly helps me become a humble person: we acquire moral virtues by first exercising them, according to Aristotle (*Nicomachean Ethics*, Book 2, Chapter 1).

Many of the virtues are means between the extremes of opposing vices: courage is between cowardice and foolhardiness, and humility lies between pride and self-humiliation. According to Aristotle all virtues have this form but this is not true of the virtue of honesty, to take just one example.

Virtue ethics allows us to qualify the maxim of impartiality that we considered earlier: the view that everybody is morally equal. Some virtues are unashamedly *partial*. I am thinking here of friendship and of many kinds of love, especially parental and marital love. Whether this partiality is a strength or a weakness in ethics is a matter of dispute (cf. Pettit, 1997, pp. 148–150; Slote, 1997, p. 228 – and Mark 3:31–34; Matthew 10:37; Luke 14:26).

EXERCISE
What do you think? Should we admire the mother's devotion to her children as much as, or more than, the charity worker's impartial benevolence?

The notion of a virtuous life is given, it is often claimed, only in a 'moral tradition' that contains 'practices' deemed good in themselves (MacIntyre, 1981). One of the advantages of virtue ethics is that it gives a 'face' to morality, which otherwise frequently seems (deliberately) theoretical and abstract. It is the face of the moral agent with a particular character, indeed of an ideal character. 'What a good person is like' is often represented in stories told within communities whose moral life is formed by such accounts (Hauerwas, 1981; Bellah, Madsen, Sullivan, Swidler and Tipton, 1985, p. 153).

Both-and ethics

Should we put all our moral eggs into the virtue basket then? Not if 'ideals of character alone cannot do all the work of ethics' (Pence, 1993, p. 254). Morality also needs principles (such as equality) and rights (such as liberty), which are not easily translated into – or eliminated by

– a concern for virtue. The instruction 'act virtuously' is not enough on its own for the moral life, if only because virtues often conflict: tactfulness with honesty, loyalty with fairness, tolerance with justice. An emphasis solely on virtue will not help us to resolve such conflicts.

Most of the moral problems we face in life, and will explore in this book, will demand an adequate ethic of obligation, for we need to know how to decide what is the right action to perform. However, questions of conduct and decision-making cannot be all that matters in ethics and particularly not in Christian ethics (cf. Galatians 5:22; Colossians 3:12–15; James 3:17). We shall also require an adequate ethic of being, which speaks of character traits, virtues and motives, and is better placed to address the perennial question of the nature of the good life for human beings.

Where obligation is supplemented in this way, virtue theory can give ethics a certain *depth*.

> On theories of duty or principle, it is theoretically possible that a person could, robot-like, obey every moral rule and lead the perfectly moral life. In this scenario, one would be like a perfectly programmed computer . . . In contrast, in virtue theory, we need to know much more than the outer shell of behaviour to make such judgements, i.e. we need to know what kind of a person is involved, how the person thinks of other people, how he or she thinks of his or her own character, how the person feels about past actions, and also how the person feels about actions not done. (Pence, 1993, p. 256)

Almost everyone goes through life without committing murder, the author continues, but there are many different *types* of non-murderer. Ethics should also be concerned with some of the ways in which they differ.

Further reading

Introductory

Hospers, J (1972), *Human Conduct: problems of ethics*, New York, Harcourt Brace Jovanovich, chapters 1 to 8.

Rachels, J (1999), *The Elements of Moral Philosophy*, Singapore, McGraw-Hill, chapters 1 and 13.

Vardy, P and Grosch, P (1994), *The Puzzle of Ethics*, London, HarperCollins, chapters 3 and 8.

Wilson, J (1961), *Reason and Morals*, Cambridge, Cambridge University Press.

Advanced

Hauerwas, S (1981), *A Community of Character: toward a constructive Christian ethic*, Notre Dame, Indiana, University of Notre Dame Press.

Skorupski, J (1996), Ethics, in N Bunnin and E P Tsui-James (eds), *The Blackwell Companion to Philosophy*, chapter 6, Oxford, Blackwell.

Slote, M (1997), Virtue ethics, in M W Baron, P Pettit and M Slote, *Three Methods of Ethics: a debate*, chapter 3, Oxford, Blackwell.

Warnock, G J (1971), *The Object of Morality*, London, Methuen.

2. MORALITY IN DEBATE

Introduction

When decisions have to be made, we sometimes discover that we hold quite strong views about what is the right thing to do. What is the basis of these views and how might we justify the rules, norms, standards or principles to which we often appeal? In this chapter we shall consider answers to these questions that are largely independent of religious claims.

> ### Reflecting on experience
> Think back to some action you once took that still appears to have been 'the right thing to do'. Then think of something you did that you (now) think was morally wrong. What *made* one of these actions right and the other one wrong, in your view?

The life game of consequences

It seems to many people that the only thing we should take into account in assessing whether an act is right or wrong is its consequences. There are two ways of thinking of consequences: one approach considers only the consequences for the agent, the other has a view of consequences that is 'agent-neutral'.

Ethical egoism

This is the claim that an action is right if it maximises (makes as great as possible) the good consequences for me; a person's duty is whatever is in that person's own interests.

> **EXERCISE**
> How would you reply to someone who thinks that he has no other
> reason for helping other people than that it is in his own interests?

In favour of this account, we might say that it allows every person to
see themselves as being of ultimate value and concern, and that many
moral principles do seem to be justified by egoism. It is, for example,
clearly to *our own* advantage (as well as theirs) not to be continually
harming other people, lying to them or breaking our promises.

But ethical egoism has many difficulties, especially when my duty to
myself (to maximise good consequences for me) conflicts with your
duty to yourself (to maximise good consequences for you). Imagine that
you are trying to kill me, because my death is in your interests. Should
I stop you? Well, stopping you would be wrong on this theory, because
under these circumstances it would be your duty to kill me. But it would
also be right, because it is in my interests that I should not die.

According to James Rachels, however, the clinching argument against
ethical egoism may be summed up in the question, 'What makes me so
special?' We noted in the last chapter that the only *moral* justification for
treating some people differently from others is that there is a morally
relevant difference between them. Just as differences such as skin
colour, gender or age do not justify our treating people differently, nothing justifies dividing the world into two unequal parts: me and the rest.

> Ethical egoism would have each person assign greater importance to
> his or her own interests than to the interests of others. But there is no
> general difference between oneself and others, to which each person
> can appeal, that justifies this difference in treatment. (Rachels, 1999,
> p. 95)

Ethical egoism is therefore 'unacceptably arbitrary'. A morality that
recognises that we are on a par with one another will demand that we
take the needs of others at least as seriously as our own. And, of course,
morality does seem to be *primarily* about our obligations to people
other than ourselves. Some would even argue that it is 'a truth about
ethics [that] one cannot have a duty, or obligation, to oneself'
(Warnock, 1998, p. 24).

Ethical egoism must be distinguished from *psychological egoism*. This
is the claim that in fact people only ever *do* act from selfish motives

(ethical egoism, by contrast, says that we *ought* only to pursue our own interests). Do we only help others as a way of proving ourselves more capable than them or because we are concerned that we might suffer the same calamity? Thomas Hobbes thought so, but his view is implausible. It is no use saying, 'People only do what they really *want* to do', for that is a tautology (it says the same thing twice). It tells us nothing about whether we might want to do something unselfish or not. Further, it is just silly to claim that 'because acting unselfishly makes us feel good, it is really selfish.' Unselfish action desires the good of others, it is satisfying when and because we achieve that end. The unselfish person is not after 'good feelings inside', she is seeking the happiness of other people (cf. Butler, 1726, sermons IX, XI). Psychological egoism would allow nobody and no behaviour *ever* to count as being unselfish.

Utilitarianism

Our next moral theory is much more plausible. The claim of utilitarianism is that an action is obligatory if it gives the best possible value, good or 'utility' – or, rather, balance of good over evil – for everyone concerned. (It is permissible if it produces at least as good a balance as any alternative action you might perform.) This is the basis of Jeremy Bentham's 'principle of utility' and John Stuart Mill's 'greatest happiness principle': ideas that powered the engines of social reform in the eighteenth and nineteenth centuries in Britain. For utilitarians, actions are again judged solely on their consequences, but now each person's welfare is treated as equally important. Sometimes utilitarians insist that we strive for 'the greatest happiness of the greatest number': maximising good for the widest population.

| Dilemma: the female spies | During World War II the British allowed a number of women intelligence agents to return to the Continent, although the War Office knew that they would be tortured and killed by the Nazis . . . If the women had not been allowed to go as planned, the Nazis would thereby have been able to infer a fact which the British were most anxious to keep secret: the fact that they had cracked the enemy's code. (Hospers, 1972, p. 223) |

EXERCISE

On utilitarian grounds, what was the right thing to do in such a situation?

What moral difficulties does the utilitarian answer present?

Utilitarianism itself comes in a number of different versions and faces a number of serious criticisms.

Is happiness the only thing of consequence? J S Mill wrote, 'happiness is desirable, and the only thing desirable, as an end; all other things being desirable as means to that end' (Mill, 1962, p. 288). But this so-called 'hedonistic' view is implausible for we value other things besides happiness. Virtue, knowledge, friendship, aesthetic enjoyment and creativity are also valued for their own sakes. For this reason, some utilitarians (or 'consequentialists') argue that the end we should pursue is 'satisfying people's preferences'.

How do we calculate consequences? If an act is made right or wrong by its consequences, where is the cut-off point? One day you save a child from drowning and fifteen years later he becomes a mass murderer. Was your action right or wrong? Perhaps we should distinguish the 'subjectively right act', the one that we conscientiously predict will give the best consequences, from the 'objectively right act', the act that actually does have the best consequences (which we can only know by hindsight: see Hospers, 1972, pp. 217–219).

Are some sorts of happiness better than others? Should our calculation take into account the quality as well as the quantity of happiness? Mill thought so, arguing that 'it is better to be a human being dissatisfied than a pig satisfied' (Mill, 1962, p. 260). But how do we balance quantity and quality: are three hours of mud-wallowing worth one hour of Mozart-listening?

Further, is it better to distribute your £5,000 lottery win equally between your one thousand friends or to restrict your giving to your closest five? Does the idea of the 'greatest number' just dilute benevolence into pointlessness?

Can the end justify the means? For many, this is the crucial question. What becomes of justice, human rights or plain personal relationships on the utilitarian view?

Dilemma: the desert island promise	I have promised a dying man on a desert island, from which subsequently I alone am rescued, to give his hoard of gold to the South Australian Jockey Club. On my return I give it to the Royal Adelaide Hospital, which, we may suppose, badly needs it for a new X-ray machine. Could anybody deny that I had done rightly without being open to the charge of heartlessness? (Remember that the promise was known only to me, and so my action will not in this case weaken the general confidence in the social institution of promising.) (Smart, 1973, p. 62)

EXERCISE
Is such an act justified? What is your reasoning here?

As we shall see in later chapters, in certain circumstances the principle of utility could justify any act provided that the consequences are good enough. It could endorse the punishment of an innocent person, the violation of an individual's rights, the overriding of the wishes of minorities or the breaking of solemn vows. But even when these actions are the means to the creation of good, can they possibly be right?

Some think that justice is built into the principle of utility, simply because everybody is 'to count for one'. But this does not appear to be the case, for two acts may both produce the same balance of good over bad consequences, even though one is patently unjust in restricting the benefit to very few. This is why the utility principle is often framed in terms of the greatest good of the greatest number. Some critics see this as combining a pure utilitarian principle with some sort of non-utilitarian principle of *distributive justice* (cf. Frankena, 1973, pp. 41–42).

What are we justifying? According to *act-utilitarianism* we should ask ourselves whether this particular act, in this particular situation, produces the best consequences. Act-utilitarians appeal to rules only as 'rules of thumb', such as 'keeping promises usually produces the greatest general good.' If the act-utilitarian estimates that in this particular situation *breaking* the promise would result in the greatest balance of good over evil, he is obliged to break that promise.

But other utilitarians (including, perhaps, Mill himself) have applied the principle of utility to rules of action, rather than separate acts. These *rule-utilitarians* say that we should keep our promises because adopting that general rule promotes the greatest good. (The act is then justified because it falls under this justified rule.) The rule-utilitarian is not always having to compute the probable effects of her actions before each decision. She just follows the general rule which, in her leisure, she has decided will produce the greatest utility if everyone followed it. Rules are far more important for the rule-utilitarian: she will obey the rule of promise-keeping, because 'always keeping promises is for the greatest general good', even in a situation where more good would be produced by breaking her promise.

EXERCISE

Do you think that rule-utilitarianism is closer to our ordinary moral viewpoint?

What criticisms do you have of it?

Is utilitarianism too impartial and demanding? A general criticism of utilitarianism is that it is actually *too* impartial, disinterested and benevolent as an account of the moral life. According to Bentham, everybody is 'to count for one, nobody for more than one' (Mill, 1962, p. 319). (In utilitarianism the agent herself is included in the calculation of the happiness of the 'greatest number', which some find morally objectionable.) But what about the special demands that our friends and families have on us? Our obligations to dependent children surely override our obligations to strangers. (Note that we can still *universalise* particular and partial principles, for instance 'If you are a parent in a situation such as this, you ought . . .')

Another problem is that utilitarianism advocates the duty of benevolence without qualification. This collapses the traditional distinction between obligations and 'acts of supererogation' (acts that go beyond what we are *required* to do). Utilitarianism just seems too demanding a moral view. Could a utilitarian justify engaging in ordinary human pursuits such as hobbies or entertainment, when he could be out 'maximising happiness'?

Christian utilitarianism? Mill thought that the ethic of Jesus was well captured in utilitarianism: 'To do as you would be done by, and to love your neighbour as yourself, constitute the ideal perfection of utilitarian morality' (Mill, 1962, p. 268). But Christian charity seems even more extreme than utilitarian altruism, in which I still count as one, for it may sometimes demand that we sell all that we have and give to the poor (Mark 10:21).

Utilitarianism defended. Supporters reject many of the criticisms of utilitarianism as irrational prejudice. They argue that it *is* sometimes justifiable to break desert island promises, to convict the innocent and even to torture someone, *in certain extreme circumstances* (cf. Smart, 1973; Pettit, 1997, pp. 150–155).

Dilemma: the new James Bond	Imagine the standard final scene of a 'Bond movie' with a twist. The dastardly megalomaniac has so arranged things that an innocent child will trigger the destruction of a whole nation by nuclear explosions if he crawls onto the pressure pad surrounding him. Bond is too far away to do anything to stop the child other than to shoot him.

EXERCISE
What should the hero do and why?

Getting in on the act itself

Many resist the attractions of utilitarianism because they believe that some actions are intrinsically right or wrong, regardless of the consequences. We should note at the outset, however, that actions are usually defined in terms of what we might call their 'immediate consequences'. Thus murder is defined as unlawful killing and is distinguished from attempted murder in which no one is actually killed. It is the *longer-term* consequences that are deemed to be irrelevant in the views we shall now consider.

EXERCISE

Choose what seems to you to be a clear candidate for an absolute moral rule or principle. Then try to think of two scenarios:
- one in which following this rule will lead to a substantial amount of unhappiness or other bad consequences;
- one in which breaking the rule will lead to a substantial amount of very good consequences.

Should we obey the rule in these cases anyway?

Philosophers have called the ethical views in this section *deontological* (from the Greek word *deon*, 'duty'), by contrast with theories such as utilitarianism which are labelled *teleological* (from the Greek word *telos*, 'goal'). On a teleological view the right is defined in terms of the good: right actions are those that give good consequences. For deontologists, the right is prior and there is no particular relationship between doing what is right and producing good results. Instead rightness is about 'acting on principle'.

Lies, promise-breaking, theft and murder are often regarded as wrong not because they produce bad consequences in a particular case or as a general rule, but because of *the types of acts they are*. So we are told that we should not perform these acts, breaking the rules that forbid them, whatever good consequences might result. Religious accounts of morality often take this line, as we shall see in the next chapter.

Deontological rules tend to be negative in form: 'Do not tell a lie' rather than 'Tell the truth.' It is possible to frame moral rules so as to capture the concerns of utilitarians and to focus on end results: for example 'Do not make people unhappy' or 'Help the needy.' But the focus here is still on obeying the rule rather than calculating consequences and (unlike rule-utilitarianism) the rules are not justified by their consequences.

Various theories have been offered to justify such moral rules, three of which are described below. More theological approaches will be treated in Chapter 3.

Formalism
For Kant and his followers, moral rules must be rational. Moral principles are rational laws that we legislate for ourselves. Kant argued that in

deciding what is right you must ask yourself whether your decision ful-
fils the formal criterion that you would be willing for everyone to follow
it. This is Kant's famous 'categorical imperative': 'act only on that
maxim through which you can at the same time will that it should
become a universal law' (Kant, 1948, p. 84). Nothing can be a moral
principle for me which cannot be a principle for everyone. Maxims
(principles on which we act) such as 'Break your promises if it suits you'
and 'Never help others in need' cannot be *universalised* in this way. It is
either inconsistent to universalise them (no one would trust a promise
under these circumstances) or their becoming a universal law would
simply be unacceptable to us.

Kant therefore lays great store on rational consistency in moral decision-making. Many would applaud this, while rejecting the apparent
implication that moral rules are abstract and without exceptions and
that there is a purely rational route to deciding what is right. 'Pay off
your credit card every month' is a maxim that cannot be universalised
(the banks would withdraw their cards), but it is not immoral.

I should caution that the proper interpretation of Kantian ethics is a
disputed area, that Kant's position is much more sophisticated than I
have suggested and that it has been robustly defended (see Baron, 1997).

Social contract theories

For others, moral rules derive from us (as on Kant's account) and have
a rational basis, but their basis is our agreement to regulate our lives by
these rules because this is to our mutual benefit. Rules are like contracts,
agreed between us by a sort of implicit moral bargaining. While on
some social contract theories the weak tend to lose out, the version of
the theory offered by John Rawls honours another aspect of Kant's
theory, that we should respect other people, treating them as 'ends in
themselves' and not solely as means (Kant, 1948, pp. 90–91). Rawls'
'contractualist' thesis constructs a story (and, of course, it is just a story)
of the negotiation of our moral duties from an 'original position' in
which no one knows what strengths, weaknesses or position in society
they will eventually possess. *Under these circumstances* (under the 'veil of
ignorance'), if we all decide what will be best for ourselves we shall need
to take account of the weak, because it might turn out that we will be
numbered among them. Self-interest and benevolence then concur.
Giving equal consideration to all ('acting impartially') seems now to be
quite reasonable: 'principles of justice may be conceived as principles
that would be chosen by rational persons' (Rawls, 1972, p. 16).

Prima facie duties

W D Ross rejected the appeal of adopting one fundamental absolute moral principle, favouring instead the messier idea of a plurality of 'prima facie duties'. For Ross there are a number of things that matter morally. These are not, however, unconditional duties that we must always perform. 'Prima facie' means 'at first sight', 'on the face of it'. Prima facie duties are only duties if no others conflict with them. But often duties do conflict and then we have to decide between them to determine what is our 'actual duty'.

EXERCISE
Look back at the desert island promise dilemma. What prima facie duties would face you in this situation?

Ross' prima facie duties are listed below (Ross, 1930, p. 21):
- duties arising because of our previous actions, including duties of keeping promises and of repairing past injuries;
- duties arising from the previous actions of others, such as the duty of gratitude to our parents;
- duties of beneficence: of promoting the greatest amount of good (as in utilitarianism);
- duties of non-maleficence: of refraining from doing harm;
- duties of justice: of distributing good equitably;
- duties of self-improvement.

Ross offers no reasons for including just these duties in the list, except that we learn them from generalising from our experience of what seems to matter in different situations. They are moral facts or truths perceived by our intuition or 'moral sense'. Ross does not attempt to rank the duties in any way either; when it comes to making a decision in a conflict-situation we just have to decide which of these principles matters most here. This is not done by applying the principles to concrete situations, but again by 'seeing' (not working out) which principle has the greatest moral relevance on balance. One of the problems with Ross' view is that conflicting principles are 'defeated', 'overturned' or 'balanced out' when we discern our actual duty in a given situation (Dancy, 1993).

Does motivation matter; is intention interesting?

You may be wondering about the role of *intention* ('one's aim or purpose in acting') in ethics; or even whether what makes an action right is not its consequences, nor the nature of the act itself, but the agent's *motive* ('what induces a person to act').

Mill remarked that 'motive has nothing to do with the morality of the action, though much with the worth of the agent' (Mill, 1962, p. 270). Some utilitarians argue that being *motivated* by impartial concern for others may not be the best route to maximising good in the world. 'If experience shows that the general happiness will be more satisfactorily attained if men frequently act from other motives than pure universal philanthropy; it is obvious that these other motives are reasonably to be preferred on Utilitarian principles' (Sidgwick, 1907, p. 413).

What about intention? If we intend good consequences but actually fail the utilitarian could say that our action was 'intended to be right'. Yet Margaret Thatcher famously remarked that 'no one would remember the Good Samaritan if he'd only had good intentions', adding 'he had money as well' (TV interview, 6 January 1986).

A distinction is often made between intending an outcome and merely foreseeing it. The principle of double effect holds that we may sometimes perform an act, provided that it is sufficiently good, even though it also has evil side effects that we foresee but do not intend. Others view this claim as 'very dubious and shifty' (Warnock, 1998, p. 30).

The deontologist will argue that you should never intentionally do something wrong, by breaking a moral rule; and indeed that you *cannot* do something wrong *unless you intend to*. Further, some acts are defined by their intention (murder, for example, and possibly terrorism). On motivation, Kant's position seems to have been that an action is *right* if it is in accordance with our duty, but only *morally good* if it is done in the recognition that it is our duty and that this is a sufficient incentive. (Whether something actually is our duty can be tested by the categorical imperative.)

For many, however, virtue ethics (see Chapter 1) gives the best account of the claim that an action is right only if it is done from a good motive, 'for the right reasons'. In admiring the generosity of the poor more than larger donations from rich people made in order to impress (cf. Mark 12:41–44), we focus on the 'inside' of a person's action rather than its 'outside': on the agent herself and her inner traits (such as kindness or generosity) rather than the overt action and its observable effects. Similarly:

We value friendship, love, and respect, and we want our relationships with people to be based on mutual regard. Acting from an abstract sense of duty, or from a desire to 'do the right thing', is not the same. We would not want to live in a community of people who acted only from such motives, nor would we want to be such a person. Therefore, the argument goes, theories of ethics that emphasize only right action will never provide a completely satisfactory account of the moral life. For that, we need a theory that emphasizes personal qualities such as friendship, love, and loyalty – in other words, a theory of the virtues. (Rachels, 1999, p. 188)

Further reading

Introductory

Gensler, H J (1998), *Ethics: a contemporary introduction*, London, Routledge, chapters 8 to 11.

Hospers, J (1972), *Human Conduct: problems of ethics*, New York, Harcourt Brace Jovanovich, chapters 9 to 17.

Mill, J S (1861), *Utilitarianism*, many editions.

Rachels, J (1999), *The Elements of Moral Philosophy*, Singapore, McGraw-Hill, chapters 5 to 11.

Singer, P (ed.) (1994), *Ethics*, Oxford, Oxford University Press, part IIB.

Advanced

Baron, M W (1997), Kantian ethics, in M W Baron, P Pettit and M Slote, *Three Methods of Ethics: a debate*, chapter 1, Oxford, Blackwell.

Singer, P (ed.) (1993), *A Companion to Ethics*, Oxford, Blackwell, part IV. (This is a very good collection of articles on ethical theories and moral problems.)

Smart, J J C and Williams, B (1973), *Utilitarianism For and Against*, Cambridge, Cambridge University Press.

3. CHRISTIAN RESOURCES

Introduction

So far we have hardly considered the subject of *Christian* ethics. This may be justified on the principle of beginning as far as possible with our own experience and reflections before entering into dialogue with the Christian tradition. In the field of morality, I would argue, the voice of our human insights and reasoning must be listened to at some length and in some depth if there is to be any genuine and intelligent conversation with the voice of the Christian moral tradition. This principle will be following in the other chapters of this book, as we explore different moral problems and issues. But first we should attune our hearing to what Christianity has to say about moral obligation and moral character.

Moral dilemmas evoke a wide variety of apparently 'moral' or 'principled' responses from people of good will, humane disposition and adequate intelligence. This is true of present-day Christians, as well as of the authors of Scripture and the Church's pronouncements down the centuries. The Christian moral tradition is a plural one.

Reflecting on experience

Has this been your experience? Try to think of examples of a moral issue concerning which there are different positions that claim to be Christian, either explicitly or by implication (for example because they are all in the New Testament).

How do you feel about – and deal with – this situation?

The variety of Christian ethics

One way of coping with plurality, of course, is to collapse it. You might want to claim that only certain positions are *really* Christian. This move from a description of the different moral positions held by people who call themselves Christian, to a 'normative' or 'prescriptive' judgement about what Christian ethics ought to be (and therefore what it 'really is'), is itself an exercise in ethical thinking. Doing Christian ethics involves more than relating the moral pronouncements of other Christians.

We can only adopt a moral position insofar as we come to agree with it and make it our own. That 'agreement' may be the result of an overwhelming moral conversion experience, in which we come to see things very differently from the way we saw them before and to accept claims that we used to reject. Nevertheless, it is *our* moral seeing, believing, acceptance and reflection that make up *our morality*. The Christian does not give up having a moral view of her own; instead she wants her own morality to be (become) Christian.

> The *Christian* part of Christian ethics comes in when the people wrestling with ethics have a faith-experience of Christ, are formed by the ethos and values of Christian tradition, are sensitive to the insights and concerns of Christian communities and, in a word, see the world with eyes which are (by their best endeavours) both human and Christlike; and, finally, that their insights are intended to benefit Christian communities, and the world through them.
>
> Put differently: if Christian ethics has any Christian specificity, it must surely be one that derives from the *faith* dimension of its practitioners' experience. (Deidun, 1998, p. 37)

The Bible and Christian ethics

Tom Deidun acknowledges the 'culture-bound' nature of the biblical writings. He illustrates this by the Old Testament's concern with purity, the early Church's disappointed eschatological views, and the fact that the biblical authors have such different ethical concerns from our own (for example over the moral significance of slavery or democracy). Their situation is simply not our situation. 'As readers of the Bible we are first of all eavesdroppers' (Deidun, 1998, p. 13) and the words of neither Jesus nor Paul can be simply transferred to our own situation. Some scholars have even argued that 'the thrust of Jesus' life and teaching was at most oblique to anything that could reasonably be called morality and not infrequently subversive of it' (Harvey, 1991, p. 32).

Deidun proposes the following broad classification of ethical approaches to the Bible.

- **A repository of divine commands:** A recognition of the diverse nature of the Bible should caution us against using it as a set of moral 'proof texts' or 'orders for the day', as should the vast number and varied nature of prescriptions in the Old Testament. In isolating divine commands from their theological, historical and literary context, this approach can trivialise and misinterpret Scripture badly.
- **An exposition of ethical ideals:** Although this is a less literalist approach, it can also ignore the diversity of Scripture in pursuit of blanket statements of master themes.
- **A source of analogies or precedents:** Deidun advocates 'an imaginative and relaxed use of biblical "analogies"' in our own life situations (p. 25).
- **A revelation of the character of God:** The main question for this approach is 'What is God doing here?' rather than 'How ought we to judge this?'
- **A formative power:** The Bible is understood here as nurturing and generating basic moral perspectives, attitudes and intentions through its images, stories and examples (cf. Brueggemann, 1996).
- **An 'informing source':** The variety of moral values and principles expressed in Scripture, addressed to a great variety of contexts, allows it to be 'one of the informing sources for moral judgments'. But Scripture is 'not sufficient in itself to make any particular judgment authoritative' (Gustafson, quoted by Deidun, 1998, p. 28).

In Deidun's view, ethics needs a more mature view of the Bible's authority, understood in terms of acknowledging its influence, potency or usefulness (relevance?) to our concerns. Paradoxically, this influence is often at its strongest when the Bible is recognised as very foreign to our world. Sometimes we need our moral thinking to be confronted by the Bible's distance from us and its 'pastness' (cf. Schweitzer, 1954, chapter XX; Nineham, 1976, pp. 196–197), so that we are jolted into seeing things differently. But this does not mean that we will see them quite in the way that any particular biblical author once saw them. The Bible is here a catalyst or disturber, not a set of solutions to moral problems that prevents us from needing to think or agonise for ourselves. (On the use and authority of the Bible in general, see two other books in this series: Evans, 1999 and Strange, 2000.)

> **EXERCISE**
> Re-read the different approaches outlined in this section. What, in your view, are the strengths and weaknesses of each?

Some themes in biblical ethics

I want now to explore some significant themes that arise out of the New Testament, before looking at general approaches to ethics in the Church's moral tradition.

The radical demands of Jesus

> **EXERCISE**
> 📖 **Read Matthew 5 to 7.**
>
> How would you characterise the main ethical features of this 'Sermon on the Mount'?

Whatever approach they take to the biblical material, most Christians will be concerned to take account of what Jesus says. But unless they adopt a fundamentalist view of Scripture and ignore the work of scholars over the last two centuries, they cannot simply read Jesus' views off the pages of the gospels. Nevertheless, something may be said with confidence about the main thrust of Jesus' teaching (cf. Borg and Wright, 1999, parts II and VIII).

'The distinctive feature of Jesus' ethical teaching is the way it radicalizes common morality' (Preston, 1993, p. 95). There are a number of dimensions to this.

• It is an 'exceeding ethic', appropriate to the generosity of a God who goes beyond what we deserve (Matthew 5:43–48; 18:21–22; Luke 10:29–37). The life demanded of the hearer-disciple should be marked by 'exceeding' but without any pride of moral or spiritual achievement (Matthew 5:20; Luke 17:10).

• It is a 'faithful ethic', based on a deep trust in a loving Father who will provide for his children. This trust releases us from the anxiety for ourselves that tends to curb generosity (Matthew 6:19–34).

• It is a 'deeper ethic', which penetrates to the deep motives of our actions, often disturbingly (Mark 7:20–23), and is highly critical of any pious morality that is merely a form of self-love or is done for show (Luke 18:9–14; Matthew 6:1–6; Mark 12:41–44).

• It is a 'reversal ethic': 'The reversal of "normal" conceptions of status and power was central . . . The Kingdom of God belongs to the poor, the outcasts, the weak, the children' (Hays, 1996, p. 167).

Jesus' radical call was a call to obedience to and trust in God (expressed in inner attitude as well as outer act), to a radical concern for the needs of and belief in the value of the neighbour (especially the outcast) and to transcend self-concern. It was often expressed in hyperbole (exaggerated language) which challenged his audience to repentance. It has been said that the precepts of Jesus were designed to 'appeal to the conscience by way of the imagination' and specify only the 'quality' and 'direction' that the disciples' acts should have in order to be genuine expressions of Christian love. They are 'not so much detailed guidance for conduct in this or that situation, as a disclosure of the absolute standards which alone are relevant when the Kingdom of God is upon us' (Dodd, 1951, pp. 60–61; cf. Chapter 4).

Jesus' teaching was directed primarily to Jews, for whom ethics would be largely a matter of obedience to the Torah, the Jewish law. His approach seems to have involved a radical new interpretation of that law, often expressed in an absolute, unqualified form, which the New Testament authors themselves sometimes make more practical and regulatory (see p. 52 below).

Because of their radical nature, some have even argued that Jesus' demands were intended as an extreme 'interim ethic' appropriate only for a brief period, as a preparation for entry into the Kingdom (Schweitzer, 1968, pp. 81–101). Martin Luther treated them as a device for generating despair, so that – convinced of our unworthiness – we throw ourselves on God's grace.

Reciprocity and the golden rule

Reciprocal behaviour is based on the principle of mutual action or 'give-and-take'; 'to reciprocate' is to return something that has been given to you (the word derives from the Latin *re* – back, *pro* – forward). We give presents and send cards at Christmas mostly to those who give to us, sometimes acknowledging that we send them 'in return'. Sociologists have suggested that complex relationships of power and obligation arise from the giving and receiving of gifts (see Bowker, 1994, pp. 12–13) and worldly-wise prudence suggests that reciprocity underlies much of our behaviour (cf. Proverbs 21:14). This is an assumption that is used to ironic effect by Jesus in Luke 16:1–10. But some gifts are given without the expectation of reciprocation, for example gifts to young children and anonymous donations to charity.

EXERCISE

📖 **Read Matthew 20:1–16; Luke 6:27–36 and 10:25–37.**

What do these passages reveal about Jesus' views on:
- God's generosity;
- our expectation of reciprocity;
- the proper relationship between God's moral nature and our actions;
- a life based on accepting God's grace in our need, rather than trying to win or deserve it through our own merit?

In the parable of the labourers in the vineyard, the payment that each worker receives (one *denarius*) was the normal daily wage of a rural worker. If the vineyard owner had paid less than this to anyone, that worker's family would have starved. The balanced reciprocity of a fair day's pay *only* being given for a fair day's work is here transcended.

Jesus' account of the character of God underscores the picture of divine generosity that is already implicit in the doctrine of creation (see Astley, 2000, chapter 2). In insisting on our 'going beyond' in response to that generosity, his teaching implies that we should exceed the limited demands of reciprocity.

📖 **Read Luke 6:31.** You might think that while the previous texts undermine the expectation of reciprocity, the *golden rule* of Luke 6:31 (and Matthew 7:12) is all about how others treat you and therefore brings reciprocity back into the picture. But that would be a mistake. The golden rule is not 'do for (and to) others as they do for (and to) you', for example by hitting back when hit, but 'treat others as you would desire and consent to being treated by others' (in the same situation, that is 'in their shoes'). This allows for a more caring, concerned and generous ethic, since we also want our neighbour's love to go beyond the calculations of give-and-take.

The golden rule prescribes behaviour that is consistent, conscientious and impartial. It has been described as:

- a workable expression of the command to love your neighbour (Luke 10:27): act to your neighbour only in ways in which you would be willing to be treated in the same situation;
- a way of counteracting self-centredness;
- a concrete application of the abstract moral notions of fairness and concern.

It is, therefore, 'a good one-sentence summary of what morality is about' (Gensler, 1998, p. 113). Do you agree?

Love says it all?
📖 Read 1 Corinthians 13.

In Christian ethics *altruism* ('devotion to the good of others') is expressed in terms of love for the neighbour. *Agape*, the word used in the Greek New Testament both for God's love and for the love demanded of us (cf. 1 John 4:7–12), is an unselfish love that does not depend on the lovableness of its object. *Agape* 'freely spends itself', bestowing itself 'on those who are not worthy of it' (Nygren, 1932, p. 165). Anders Nygren regards this gift-love as incompatible with *eros* (need-love), which is 'a will to have and to possess, resting on a sense of need'.

However, our love for others will never be without elements of passion and need satisfaction, nor should it be, although *agape* can transform them as we come to love our neighbour 'for his own sake' and 'on her own behalf', and not solely for our fulfilment (cf. Lewis, 1963; Brümmer, 1993). Stanley Grenz argues that we need an ethic of love that is more comprehensive than *agape* alone, lest that degenerate into passionless self-giving for the sake of duty. 'True care', he writes, 'involves an *agape* infused with the emotional tones represented in other dimensions of love', including familial concern and friendship as well as desire (Grenz, 1997, p. 293).

Such love is *active concern* and service, a matter of the will rather than just affection. It may lead to self-sacrifice (Mark 10:21; John 15:12–13) but even then it is the neighbour who is important, not our own loss of self. As the command is to love your neighbour 'as yourself' (Leviticus 19:18; Luke 10:27; Romans 13:9), it is incompatible with hating or despising ourselves.

Love, the greatest of the 'theological virtues' and the 'more excellent way' (1 Corinthians 12:31), may be expressed in an ethic of action *and* an ethic of character. In Christian ethics both are modelled on the ministry and person of Christ. Paul's great hymn to love has been described as a portrait for which Jesus is the sitter.

The imitation of Christ

Israel is called to be holy as God is holy (Leviticus 19:2) and the disciples are to be perfect 'as your heavenly Father is perfect' (Matthew 5:48). Christ himself is the image of God (2 Corinthians 4:4; Colossians 1:15) and may therefore serve as a model, as may those who imitate him (1 Corinthians 11:1). The whole life of the Christian is to be modelled on the pattern of humiliation, suffering and triumph of the Christ event (Philippians 2:1–11). Discipleship itself is a way of imitation or 'following', as the apprentice-disciple learns from the master-teacher's life, which is his lived-out ethic, as well as from his words (cf. Mark 10:21; John 13:12–17; 1 Peter 2:22).

Christians are not, however, to seek any superficial tailoring of their life to reflect his life, nor is their individual responsibility and freedom to be quenched through this imitation. Rather, they are to exercise the spiritual maturity, insight and moral wisdom of those who have the 'mind of Christ' (1 Corinthians 2:14–16).

> Such a morality does not consist in conformity to any stereotyped pattern; it consists rather in learning from Jesus an attitude of mind which comprises sensitivity to the presence of God and to the will of God which is the only authority, a constant submission of personal interest to the pursuit of that will in the well-being of others, and a confidence that, whatever the immediate consequences may appear to be, the outcome can safely be left in God's hands. (Caird, 1994, p. 203)

This *imitatio Christi* theme fits best with an ethic of character or virtue; the will of God being discerned through a transformed mind and disposition. It is not the admiration of a distant ideal; for Paul (Romans 6:4; 2 Corinthians 3:18):

> imitation comes from participation: Christian love, service and hunger for justice expresses the very life that is within those who have been plunged into Christ. They are not merely friends of Christ; they have become part of his living Body. (Spohn, 1999, p. 150; cf. chapter 7)

EXERCISE
The sections on love and on the imitation of Christ illustrate a
Christian ethic that speaks of Christian character rather than just
Christian obligation. Look back at the taxonomy of ethical
approaches to the Bible at the beginning of this chapter. Which
approaches fit best an ethic of duty and which place more stress on
the revelation of ideals of character or virtue?

Morality and reward

Even a cursory reading of Scripture reveals a concern for rewards and
punishment.

EXERCISE
📖 Read Exodus 20:12; Deuteronomy 5:32–33; Luke 14:7–11;
Matthew 19:29 and 25:31–46.

How do you understand this theology of rewards?

Although the New Testament does not regard these rewards as material, and its underlying theology is of God's grace rather than human
merit or desert (cf. Luke 17:10), many feel that this dimension conflicts
with other aspects of Christian ethics. In particular, reward and punishment seem incompatible with the encouragement of selfless love and
the teaching that virtue should be done for the sake of the other, for
God's sake or for its own sake, and not – or never solely – for the sake
of the virtuous person's own well-being.

The texts are open to other interpretations, but you might argue that
Jesus' stress on motive is not so much an endorsement of our striving
for purity of heart as of our acting for love's sake, often unselfcon-
sciously. Ronald Preston reminds us that in the allegory of the sheep
and the goats, the sheep are unconscious of either their goodness or of
rewards. 'The thrust of the teaching is towards a self-forgetfulness which
results in an unselfconscious goodness. Writers on spirituality call it disinterestedness' (Preston, 1993, p. 96).

Disinterestedness is not the same as a lack of attention or concern;

the word means absence of *self-interest*, in the sense of personal benefit or advantage. Logically, disinterestedness cannot be pursued directly. Religion at its best insists that we are to concentrate on the other, not on our own souls or their possible ultimate reward. To say that 'giving is its own reward' is to say that giving does not seek any reward, that giving is not a means to something further but an end in itself. Hence 'treasure in heaven is the treasure you acquire by not being interested in acquiring any treasure.' In the New Testament, Gareth Moore argues, 'the language of rewards is being used in order to encourage people to forget all about rewards' (Moore, 1988, pp. 165, 145; cf. pp. 151, 169).

'Traditional' approaches to Christian ethics

In Chapter 2 we explored various senses in which an action, or the rules that govern it, might be judged right or wrong 'of itself' quite apart from its consequences. In this chapter we meet two popular *theological* approaches to this issue from the Christian tradition.

Revealed commands

The 'divine command theory' identifies the moral good with God's will and what is right with what God commands. Ethics is obedience to the command of God. This is a natural viewpoint for religions that claim access to a revelation of God's will; within the Christian tradition it has been particularly influential among Protestants. For Karl Barth, the task of Christian ethics is to respond to God's command even though no human ethical theory will ever fully capture it.

The major problem with this general approach is that of knowing what God commands and forbids, even in the moral area. As we saw earlier, appeal to the Bible is problematic in the field of morality and God commands many things in Scripture that we take to be no part of morality. The (more Catholic) suggestion that we should listen in addition to God's revelation in Christian history and the Church's teaching adds to the difficulty of discerning God's authentic voice among such a range of opinions. The (more liberal) claim that God's will may be found through the Christian's exercise of reason, or through her own moral experience or intuition, seems little different from *non-religious* ways of discovering what we ought to do. Barth, by contrast, insists that God's command for any individual case comes through a specific gracious act of God, which we must listen to seriously and obediently (Barth, 1961, p. 27).

Natural law

The Catholic tradition appeals to a 'natural law', in addition to any supernaturally revealed moral rules. The theory of natural law emphasises the role of reason in moral decision-making.

Thomas Aquinas' notion of natural law is similar to views held by Aristotle and Cicero. It claims that what one ought to do is somehow based on the sort of beings we are and the changes that are natural to us. Aquinas argued that 'all things are regulated and measured by Eternal Law' and somehow share in it, 'in that their tendencies to their own proper acts and ends are from its impression'. However, unlike the animals (which express their own God-given nature unconsciously and instinctively), we can think about our nature and ask ourselves, 'What is human nature *for?*' and 'How can its purpose (*telos* or "end") best be achieved?' 'Now this sharing in the Eternal Law by intelligent creatures is what we call "natural law"', Aquinas writes.

The basis of natural law theory therefore rests on the claim that we can discover by unaided reason how we should behave, since we ought to behave in a way that promotes God's intentions in his creation as shown in God's design of our nature. In a sense, then, morality is to be found in human nature and 'the light of natural reason by which we discern what is good and what evil, is nothing but the impression of divine light on us' (Aquinas, *Summa Theologiae*, 1a2ae, 91, 2; Vol. 28, 1996, p. 23).

Protestant moral theology has criticised this account for ignoring the doctrine of the Fall and underestimating the extent to which human disobedience has resulted in a distortion and weakening of human reason and human nature. Thus John Calvin recognised a natural law known by conscience (which is the basis for civil law) but argued that this is confused by sin and needs the illumination of the written law of God. Protestant theology frequently asserts that, without God's grace, 'unaided reason' cannot discover divine truth, even moral truth. Many argue that we should give up all attempts to discover for ourselves how we should behave and simply listen to God's revelation through Scripture.

But those who accept a stronger view of natural reason claim that it can discover both the purpose of human nature and the rules by which we should live in order to fulfil our human *telos*. At the most basic level, these rules are:
- to do good and avoid evil;
- to preserve human life;

- to propagate the species; and
- to promote human society.

EXERCISE

How do you react to the claims of natural law theory? What other criticisms might it face?

Although the basic principles of natural law are mainly non-controversial, difficulties arise when these general principles are applied to specific cases or when they conflict. Controversial secondary precepts that have been derived from the basic rules include prohibitions of euthanasia and artificial birth control (see Chapters 4 and 5).

A more fundamental problem, and one beyond the scope of this book, is whether this is a legitimate way of deriving an 'ought' (what we ought to do) from an 'is' (what Nature is like and what is natural for us). David Hume was critical of all attempts to leap from factual description to moral valuation; others have been particularly critical of a morality that endorses 'Nature's way' as showing us what ought to happen and how we ought to behave. Nevertheless, natural law theory at least tries to keep our (God-given and common) human nature central to our ethical reflections.

Practical Christian ethics

Christian ethics, like other moral systems, tends to propound general rules, laws, duties and maxims which have to be applied to particular, often complex and ambiguous case-situations. *Casuistry* is the term used for the art of deciding what is right or wrong in particular cases, beginning from insufficiently precise general rules such as 'Thou shalt not kill' or 'Preserve life.'

Middle axioms are said to lie intermediate between universal principles or moral aims and specific situations. They are often couched in terms of provisional maxims of behaviour or realisable objectives of moral endeavour, for example achieving democracy or abolishing racial discrimination. They lie close to Paul Ramsey's *summary rules*, obtained by generalising from particular actions ('reports that cases of a certain sort have been found to be most love-fulfilling'), and his *rules of practice*, which derive from the justification of a practice as a whole (for example fidelity in marriage and promise-keeping in business) (Ramsey, 1967, chapter VI). This second category bears an obvious similarity to the rule-utilitarianism we looked at in the last chapter.

Situation (or contextual) ethics, by contrast, begins with the concrete moral situation and regards no rule as intrinsically valid and universal. Every situation must be judged by us on its own merits. Joseph Fletcher writes, 'It all depends on the situation. What is right in one case . . . may be wrong in another case . . . There is only one thing that is always good and right, intrinsically good regardless of the context, and that one thing is love' (Fletcher, 1966, pp. 59–60). This approach appears similar to act-utilitarianism; but it might also be understood in terms of some sort of intuition into what is the most loving thing to do in a given situation, or as advocating acting from the motive of love (cf. Fletcher, 1966, pp. 26–31, 134–145; Lehmann, 1963, chapter 5).

EXERCISE

What is your view of the value and status of rules in Christian ethics?

Can we do without them?

Working it out in Christ

I conclude with a suggestion of how to handle a specific moral case (Advisory Council for the Church's Ministry, 1974, appendix 4; cf. Cook, 1983, chapter 4).

First, find out about the circumstances in which the moral decision has to be made (What is the real problem here? What are the attitudes and motives of those involved? What are the foreseeable consequences? What else do we need to know?).

Second, find out what relevant insights are available (from the Bible and Christian tradition, and the 'general or common moral wisdom of the community').

Third, form an opinion, based on these facts and values, about what should be done (and ask the opinion of those involved in the situation).

Finally, develop this insight into a considered judgement. Ask yourself: Is it grounded in moral reasoning? Is it a Christian position? Is your moral judgement distinguishable from any technical, factual assessment? 'Have you distinguished between what is desirable and what is possible?' Have you done justice to conflicting claims? Is your proposed line of action acceptable to the people in this situation? What other factors might have influenced your decision – and are they relevant to it?

Further reading

Introductory

Advisory Council for the Church's Ministry (1974), *Teaching Christian Ethics: an approach*, London, SCM.

Attwood, D (1998), *Changing Values: how to find moral truth in modern times*, Carlisle, Paternoster.

Brown, D (1983), *Choices: ethics and the Christian*, Oxford, Blackwell.

Cook, D (1983), *The Moral Maze: a way of exploring Christian ethics*, London, SPCK.

Davies, D (1994), Christianity, in J Holm and J Bowker (eds), *Making Moral Decisions*, chapter 2, London, Cassell.

Fletcher, J (1966), *Situation Ethics: the new morality*, London, SCM.

Higginson, R (1988), *Dilemmas: a Christian approach to moral decision making*, London, Hodder and Stoughton.

Jones, R G (1984), *Groundwork of Christian Ethics*, London, Epworth.

McDonald, J I H (1995), *Christian Values: theory and practice in Christian ethics today*, Edinburgh, T and T Clark.

Advanced

Dunstan, G R (ed.) (1975), *Duty and Discernment*, London, SCM.

Grenz, S J (1997), *The Moral Quest: foundations of Christian ethics*, Leicester, Apollos.

Hoose, B (1994), *Received Wisdom? Reviewing the role of tradition in Christian ethics*, London, Chapman.

Hoose, B (ed.) (1998), *Christian Ethics: an introduction*, London, Cassell, part I. (This book contains a very good collection of articles on different areas of Christian ethics.)

Houlden, J L (1973), *Ethics and the New Testament*, Harmondsworth, Penguin.

Keeling, M (1990), *The Foundations of Christian Ethics*, Edinburgh, T and T Clark.

McDonald, J I H (1993), *Biblical Interpretation and Christian Ethics*, Cambridge, Cambridge University Press.

Spohn, W C (1999), *Go and Do Likewise: Jesus and ethics*, New York, Continuum.

White, R E O (1994), *Christian Ethics*, Leominster, Gracewing.

Wogaman, J P (1976), *A Christian Method of Moral Judgment*, London, SCM.

4. WHAT IS A LIFE WORTH?

Introduction

We move now to consider a range of moral issues, concentrating in this chapter on the beginning and end of life.

Reflecting on experience
Reflect on what you think about abortion and euthanasia, using these opinion poll questions.

Q1. Do you approve or disapprove of **abortion** under the following circumstances? *Please tick the appropriate box.*

	Approve	Disapprove	Don't know
(a) Where the mother's health is at risk by the pregnancy	❑	❑	❑
(b) Where it is likely that the child would be born physically handicapped	❑	❑	❑
(c) Where the woman is not married	❑	❑	❑
(d) Where a married couple do not want to have any more children	❑	❑	❑

Q2. Do you approve or disapprove of **euthanasia** under the following circumstances? *Please tick the appropriate box.*

	Approve	Disapprove	Don't know
(a) Where someone has a painful incurable illness and has requested euthanasia	❑	❑	❑
(b) Where someone is not ill but is simply tired of life and has requested euthanasia	❑	❑	❑
(c) Where a terminally ill person on a life support machine is comatose and likely to remain so	❑	❑	❑

How do your own views compare with those of the general population? MORI polls show a decline in those who thought that it was wrong for unmarried women to have abortions, from 38% in 1983 to 21% in 1996 (with 65% rejecting this view). The results from recent surveys show that over 90% of Anglican weekly churchgoers approved of abortion in case (a) of Q1 above and 82% in case (b). However, less than a third approved of abortion on purely financial grounds (Gill, 1999, pp. 182–183). Among younger populations, Francis and Kay's study of 13- to 15-year-olds shows that 50% of weekly churchgoers, but only 35% of the non-churchgoers, believe that 'abortion is wrong' (Francis and Kay, 1995, p. 87).

We shall explore attitudes to euthanasia later in the chapter.

Abortion

One in three British women have had an abortion before the age of thirty-five. Nevertheless, debate over the morality of artificially terminating a pregnancy continues unabated, often focused on the competing rights of the pregnant woman and her unborn child (technically an 'embryo' up to eight weeks after conception and a 'foetus' thereafter).

In Britain abortions are legal, usually up to the twenty-fourth week of pregnancy, provided that two doctors agree that continuing the pregnancy would result in:
- a greater risk to the life (in which case there is no time limit), or the mental or physical health, of the mother than termination would pose;
- an adverse affect, again greater than the risk of termination, on the mental or physical health of existing children; or
- a risk that the baby will be born with a 'serious' physical or mental handicap (again, in this case there is no time limit).

Some argue that the 1967 Abortion Act (revised in 1990), in referring to the 'mental health of the pregnant woman or any existing children' and allowing that 'account may be taken of the pregnant woman's . . . environment', could be said to permit abortion solely on the grounds that she does not want the child or that it would be better for her family if she did not have it.

Decisions over abortion often seem to be made on some form of utilitarian calculation: balancing the overall happiness of the baby, and the happiness it may cause to others, against that of the mother (and others involved). Then the question is: Will the world overall be a happier place if this child is born or not?

The notion of rights, it is claimed, forbids such calculations (see Chapter 8) and the *right to life* is the main area of dispute over abortion. However, some argue that rights may be infringed in extreme cases, particularly if rights conflict, and we then have to decide if these particular circumstances are extreme enough. This view seems to empty the notion of a right to life of much of its power.

There is little argument over the right to life of a newly-born infant but how far back into pregnancy does that right extend? Some think that everything depends on when the developing embryo-foetus becomes a 'person', suggesting criteria such as brain activity, 'sentience' (the capacity to have experiences), viability outside the womb, rationality or capacity for relationships. However, opponents of abortion may speak even of the fertilised egg as a 'potential person'.

EXERCISE

Perhaps we should argue that 'being a person is a matter of degree'. On this account, 'a one-year-old is much more of a person than a new-born baby or a foetus just before birth, but each of these is more of a person than the embryo' (Glover, 1977, pp. 127–128). How do you respond to this view? What are its implications?

A number of related questions arise in this debate.

- Has every living human being a right to life, however incapacitated mentally or physically? Is this a *religious* belief about the 'sanctity' of human life, which derives from the claim that God has created humans with a special status and value?

- Some have argued that 'there is nothing intrinsically good in a person merely being alive and that the idea of a "right to life" should be rejected' (Glover, 1977, p. 138). It is not life itself which is worth preserving but life of a certain quality – 'worth-while life'. Some would argue that the life of severely handicapped children is 'not worth living'. And yet 'there are people in possession of all their faculties who seem to be very unhappy indeed and people in possession of very few faculties who give an impression of considerable happiness and are very much loved by those around them' (Keeling, 1970, p. 70).

Below are two very different arguments producing diametrically opposite conclusions.

Remember mother

According to Harry Gensler, we are forced to take an anti-abortion view in order to be morally consistent. He appeals to the golden rule of treating others as you would (now) consent to being treated, or to having been treated, in the same situation (see Chapter 3). Gensler writes:

> **Dilemma: considering abortion**
>
> Suppose that you're a pregnant woman. You're about to abort the foetus. But you ask yourself, 'How do I react to the idea of my mother having aborted me under such circumstances?' If you kill the unborn, and yet don't consent to the idea of your mother having done the same thing to you in the same situation, then you violate the golden rule and are inconsistent. (Gensler, 1998, pp. 184–185)

EXERCISE

If you have been pregnant and have agonised over whether you ought to have the baby or not, this discussion will seem very cool and clinical. But reflecting carefully is also a form of caring: caring about the truth and about what is right. So, what do you make of Gensler's argument against abortion?

Consider the following questions.

• Does golden rule reasoning not also support a very different position: that as an adviser, parent or doctor you should enable or encourage a pregnant woman's abortion if you would want to have an abortion in the same situation? (Gensler argues that we can act consistently, following the golden rule, but still act wrongly; the golden rule does not tell us what specific action to do: Gensler, 1998, pp. 110–112.)

• If it would have been wrong for your parents to have aborted you, would it also have been wrong for them not to have conceived you in the first place? Gensler replies that we can will a general prohibition against aborting but not against non-conceiving (think of the results!).

• Might you have agreed 'not to have been born' (cf. Jeremiah 20:14–18; Job 3) if you knew you would be severely handicapped, in continual pain or short-lived? Might you even have agreed not to be born because your birth would adversely affect, or even destroy, your mother's life?

Gensler, by the way, holds that abortion is *normally* wrong (and that it is *seriously* wrong) but admits that his reasoning does not allow that it is *always* wrong (p. 188).

Whose body is it anyway?

Judith Jarvis Thomson offers a very different perspective. She asks us to consider whether a person's right to life (and therefore the right to life of a foetus, if a foetus is a person) is stronger and more stringent than the mother's right to determine what shall happen in her own body. She tells this story.

Dilemma: unplugging the violinist

You wake up in the morning and find yourself back to back in bed with . . . a famous unconscious violinist. He has been found to have a fatal kidney ailment, and the Society of Music Lovers has canvassed all the available medical records and found that you alone have the right blood type to help. They have therefore kidnapped you, and last night the violinist's circulatory system was plugged into yours, so that your kidneys can be used to extract poisons from his blood, as well as your own. The director of the hospital now tells you, 'Look, we're sorry the Society of Music Lovers did this to you – we would never have permitted it if we had known. But still, they did it, and the violinist now is plugged into you. To unplug you would be to kill him. But never mind, it's only for nine months. By then he will have recovered from his ailment, and can safely be unplugged from you.' (Thomson, 1975, pp. 90–91)

EXERCISE

Thomson asks, 'Is it morally incumbent on you to accede to this situation?' How would you answer and how relevant is this story to your views on abortion?

• Does another person's right to life *always* outweigh your right to decide what happens to your body? Thomson writes, 'A woman surely can defend her life against the threat to it posed by the unborn child, even if doing so involves its death' (p. 94).

• In the story, 'the violinist has no right against you that *you* shall allow him to continue to use your kidneys' (p. 97) because you gave him no such right. It would therefore not be unjust to unplug him. But perhaps you ought to do something for another person, even when that person has no right to it? You may think that you have a special responsibility for *your* baby; but is that true even if you always carefully used contraception or you were raped? Thomson insists, 'Surely we do not have any such "special responsibility" for a person unless we have assumed it, explicitly or implicitly' (p. 105).

Christian and biological perspectives

All the Churches view abortion as a morally serious matter. Anglican and mainstream Protestant Churches allow that abortion may be justified under certain circumstances. Many 'pro-life' campaigners, however, hold fundamentalist Protestant views. Although the Bible does not mention abortion directly, it says that God forms us in the womb (Psalm 139:13; Jeremiah 1:5), it contains injunctions against murder and it expresses concern for the weak and defenceless.

EXERCISE
📖 **Read Exodus 21:12–25.**

Does the Old Testament law treat the foetus differently from a person?

It would appear so. The penalty for murder (premeditated, intentional killing) is death, but causing a miscarriage (here the intention is uncertain) only leads to a fine, unless the *mother* is injured.

In the Christian tradition the first clear teaching on the subject of abortion comes from the second century *Didache*, which condemns the practice (2:2). Christian theologians and Church councils have usually taken the same view. However, Augustine made a distinction between abortions taking place before, and those administered after, the 'animation' of the foetus when it received its soul (variously estimated at 40, 60 or 80 days). Aquinas held that the foetus cannot have a human soul until it develops a recognisably human shape, a view affirmed by the

Council of Vienne (1311–1312). In the seventeenth century this shape was mistakenly 'seen' through primitive microscopes in the fertilised egg itself. Forty years ago, an Anglican professor of pastoral theology declared, 'both biologists and theologians are now generally agreed in regarding the living foetus as a human being . . . from the moment of conception. If that is so, then it must be held sacred from that moment' (Wood, 1961, p. 55). But at what stage in the continuous and gradual development of the embryo-foetus we should treat it in the way that we treat other human beings remains a highly contentious issue. 'Human life' begins before conception, of course, as both sperm and eggs are human and alive; but sentience does not develop for some time and the foetus is capable of being born alive only after about twenty-three weeks.

The Roman Catholic Church now teaches that to kill an unborn child directly and intentionally at any stage is wrong. The double effect doctrine, however, allows the death of a foetus as an inevitable consequence of a medical intervention to save the mother's life (for example by removing a cancerous uterus).

Most Christians would resist the view that abortion is morally neutral and may therefore be permitted on demand. However, some would argue that before the foetus is fourteen days old (the time when the primitive streak that forms the beginning of the nervous system develops and when implantation in the womb happens), such a view *is* acceptable. Unfortunately, most women would not know they were pregnant such a short time after conception. Abortion is always to be viewed as at least 'a pity' (Warnock, 1998, p. 52) or as a grave moral decision involving a serious moral cost, even though it may be morally justifiable in certain circumstances. Such a decision should not be made lightly; but perhaps it may be made.

What do you think?

Euthanasia

The word euthanasia means 'good death' and labels an easy or gentle death. When we see people in a painful terminal illness, especially those close to us, we often wish that we could engineer such a death for them. But is killing others, or assisting their suicide, ever morally justified?

Some would claim that it is, even where the patient cannot request it – as in the case of long-term comatose patients in a 'permanent vegetative state' or severely handicapped people. The debate on euthanasia has mostly centred on the 'easier' moral issue of *voluntary euthanasia*, however, where the patient requests such killing or 'physician-assisted suicide'. Both practices are permitted in the Netherlands, while remaining officially illegal there (as in Britain and most other countries); assisted suicide is currently legal in Oregon.

Look back now to your responses to Q2 of the questionnaire. The British Social Attitudes surveys in the mid 1990s showed over 80% of the general population in favour of allowing euthanasia for the terminally ill, although only 45% of weekly churchgoers took this view. On euthanasia, as with abortion, Anglican churchgoers are less likely to hold traditional moral views than are Roman Catholics, and a clear majority of Anglicans approve of euthanasia for the terminally ill (Gill, 1999, pp. 184–186). Euthanasia for permanently comatose, terminally ill patients is supported by 86% of the general population but only 12% endorse euthanasia for those who are simply 'tired of life'.

Advances in medicine and in the technology of life-supporting machines mean that many seriously ill or handicapped people can now be kept alive who would have quickly died a few years ago. The fact that many painkilling drugs shorten life allows individual doctors to escape prosecution with the defence that a hastened death was an (unintended but not unforeseen) side effect of patient care, on the argument from double effect.

Dilemma: the brothers	Matthew Donnelly ... contracted cancer and lost part of his jaw, his upper lip, his nose, and his left hand, as well as two fingers from his right hand. He was also left blind. Mr Donnelly's physicians told him that he had about a year to live, but he decided that he did not want to go on living in such a state. He was in constant pain – one writer said that 'at its worst, he could be seen lying in bed with teeth clenched and beads of perspiration standing out on his forehead.' Knowing that he was going to die eventually anyway, and wanting to escape this misery, Mr Donnelly begged his three brothers to kill him. (Rachels, 1999, p. 99)

EXERCISE
If you were one of Matthew's brothers, what would you have done?

You may be willing to give some weight to the following points.

- Utilitarians insist that the overall benefit must first be calculated. This involves balancing the patient's life and happiness against his pain and suffering. (But how do you balance life against *anything* else?) It also involves taking into account the cost to others, including the monetary and emotional cost, of maintaining or ending this life.
- It is often said that we put too much stress on the quantity (length) of life when the quality of life is really what matters: its achievements, joys, relationships and creations (particularly of good for others).
- Does an individual not have the right to determine the end of his own life? Despite religious reservations, many would say that this is *our* ultimate 'right to life'. But do we 'own' our lives?
- Is my concern for the sufferer in part a mask for my self-interest about my own peace of mind and sense of helplessness?
- We feel obliged to put animals 'out of their suffering'. Is it just an over-scrupulous concern with our own purity that prevents our performing this last act of kindness in the case of apparently pointless human pain and suffering?

In fact, two of Matthew Donnelly's brothers refused to kill him, but his youngest brother, 36-year-old Harold, took a pistol into the hospital and shot him dead. He was arrested and charged with murder.

The wider picture

Debates about euthanasia are usually not so starkly personal. Proponents of the legalisation of voluntary euthanasia are often told to look at the wider situation rather than individual hard cases. How do you respond to the following points?

- In recent years the Hospice Movement has shown that terminal illness and death can be experienced in a context of love, dignity and a minimum of pain.
- If voluntary euthanasia were legalised, many ill people might feel at least a moral pressure that they ought to submit to it so as to prevent the suffering of their families and carers.
- Another utilitarian argument against legalising euthanasia is that its practice would undermine our trust in the medical profession and that profession's own sense that its doctors and nurses must always act to preserve life. (The abortion debate sometimes appeals to a similar argument.)
- If voluntary euthanasia were legalised, the 'slippery slope' effect might result in society condoning *involuntary* euthanasia of the handi-

capped, 'racially impure' or political opponents. (Is this a *moral* argument, however, or just a *factual* claim about human nature and the abuse of power?)

Christian perspectives
📖 Read Psalm 100:3 and 1 Samuel 31:1–6.

As in the case of abortion and suicide, Christians often appeal to the notion that life is a sacred gift from God. But unlike other gifts, we do not absolutely own our own life and therefore cannot do just what we want with it. Especially, we cannot destroy it. Suicide, and therefore voluntary euthanasia, is a rejection of the creator's gift of life – an act of rebellious disobedience that precludes repentance. This religious argument is perhaps better expressed in terms of life as a *loan* and our responsibilities as 'stewards' of creation.

Initially neutral or even positive (as in 2 Maccabees), the Jewish view on suicide later turned to repugnance and condemnation (Tobit 3:7–17 and Josephus, 1981, pp. 218–219). The New Testament refers to Judas' suicide (Matthew 27:5) but is as non-committal as the Old Testament on the general issue. Augustine utterly condemned suicide, including it under killing forbidden by the sixth commandment. According to natural law theory, it was seen as contrary to human nature. Aquinas argued that it was for God to decide when life should end.

While describing any *action* causing death as a relief from suffering as 'a grave violation of the law of God', Pope John Paul II also argued, in his encyclical *Evangelium Vitae* (1995), that 'extraordinary' care or medical treatment to prolong life need not be continued if it is futile, dangerous or burdensome to the patient, family or society. In many States such a withdrawal of care is legal. The administering of drugs such as morphine with the intention to prevent pain, even when they hasten death, was also accepted by the Pope in some circumstances, by appeal to the doctrine of double effect. The concern throughout is that there should be no *direct* attack on human life. A similar position was taken by the House of Bishops of the Church of England in 1992.

However, Christians have traditionally praised those martyrs who allowed themselves to be killed. A terminally ill patient who wishes to die so as to prevent further hardships being inflicted on his family and carers may be seen as intending a similarly noble act. After all, 'No one has greater love than this, to lay down one's life for one's friends' (John 15:13). What do you think?

Further reading

Introductory

General Synod Board for Social Responsibility (2000), *On Dying Well: a contribution to the euthanasia debate*, London, Church House Publishing.

General Synod Board for Social Responsibility (1993), *Abortion and the Church: what are the issues?* London, Church House Publishing.

Cook, D (1983), *The Moral Maze: a way of exploring Christian ethics*, London, SPCK, chapters 5 and 6.

Crawford, R (2000), *Can We Ever Kill?* London, Darton, Longman and Todd, chapters 2 and 3.

Singer, P (1993), *Practical Ethics*, Cambridge, Cambridge University Press.

Trowell, H (1973), *The Unfinished Debate on Euthanasia*, London, SCM.

Advanced

Banner, M (1999), *Christian Ethics and Contemporary Moral Problems*, Cambridge, Cambridge University Press, chapters 2 and 3.

Dworkin, R (1993), *Life's Dominion: an argument about abortion, euthanasia and individual freedom*, New York, Knopf.

Gill, R (ed.) (1998), *Euthanasia and the Churches*, London, Cassell.

Pojman, L P and Beckwith, F J (eds) (1995), *The Abortion Controversy*, London, Jones and Bartlett.

Rachels, J (1986), *The End of Life: euthanasia and morality*, Oxford, Oxford University Press.

5. SEX AND SOCIETY

Introduction

The notion of 'sin', in origin a purely theological word labelling rebellious disobedience to God, has become debased in common parlance by restricting its application solely to sexual misdemeanours ('living in sin'). The Churches themselves frequently seem as obsessed with sex as do the tabloid newspapers. The only excuse for all this is that our sexuality is fundamental to our human nature and its expression is a powerful driving force for good or ill in some of our closest relationships. As such, it has had a profound effect on society.

The last century saw a major revolution in sexual attitudes and behaviour, from which the Christian Church has not been isolated and to which it has been forced to respond.

Reflecting on experience
Reflecting on your own experience of human relationships and your own moral views, how would you respond to these questions from opinion surveys?

Q3. If a man and a woman have **sexual relations before marriage**, what would your general opinion be? *Please tick the appropriate box.*

Always Wrong	Mostly Wrong	Sometimes Wrong	Rarely Wrong	Not Wrong At All	Depends/ Varies	Don't Know
❑	❑	❑	❑	❑	❑	❑

Q4. Do you agree or disagree that (*please tick one box on each line*):

	Agree Strongly	Agree	Neither Agree nor Disagree	Disagree	Disagree Strongly	Can't Choose
(a) Married people are generally happier than unmarried people	❑	❑	❑	❑	❑	❑
(b) People who want children ought to be married	❑	❑	❑	❑	❑	❑
(c) A single mother can bring up her child as well as can a married couple	❑	❑	❑	❑	❑	❑

Opinion poll answers to questions about sex before marriage have changed dramatically over recent decades. In 1964, 64% of the general British population polled by Gallup disapproved of sex before marriage; by 1978 the proportion was down to 26%. In a different survey, 28% said that pre-marital sex was 'always' or 'mostly wrong' in 1983; by 1993 this figure had fallen to 18%. Churchgoers are more likely to disapprove, yet a Gallup Poll in 1996 found that the majority (56%) of adult churchgoing Anglicans now thought that it was right for a couple to live together without intending to get married.

On the whole, people still tend to endorse more traditional responses to Q4(b) above, but the percentage who 'agree strongly' or 'agree' to this proposition has also declined over recent years, and was down to 57% in 1994. However, 87% of weekly churchgoers endorsed this view then, compared with only 40% of those with no religion (Gill, 1999, pp. 156–158).

Data from the *British Social Attitudes* survey of 1989 show that over 30% of respondents believed that a lone mother can bring up children as well as a couple (Q4(c)). However, over 50% disagreed with this claim. Although it is often said that married people are happier, on average, than the unmarried, divorced or widowed (Argyle, 1987, pp. 16–17), only 24% of the general population 'agreed' or 'strongly agreed' with Q4(a) in the survey of 1994.

Sex and sin

The idea that the body is inferior to and separable from the soul, viewed as the spiritual and rational part of a human being, is to be found in Greek thought but not in the Bible. The biblical doctrine of creation recognises the goodness of all things, matter included, and treats human beings as a unity of mind and body: we are essentially and naturally embodied, but not imprisoned, in our flesh (see Astley 2000, chapters 2 and 9). Jewish thinking has usually celebrated sex and family life.

Nevertheless, Paul is cautious about sex, even within marriage:

EXERCISE

📖 **Read 1 Corinthians 7:1–10, 25–38.**

How do you react to Paul's views on sex and marriage?

Are there particular first-century circumstances that might have influenced him?

Paul wrote, in the expectation of an imminent second coming of Christ and end of history, to a Church whose views on the body were more Greek than Jewish. This may explain why his position, that 'marriage is permitted, but is not therefore necessarily advisable' (Barrett, 1971, p. 186), is less whole-hearted than that of his Scriptures (cf. Genesis 2:18).

Later Christian thought further downplayed both sex and the family. On the *purpose* of human sexuality, the Christian tradition has often followed Augustine:

> Instead of maintaining the goodness of the sexual instinct in *itself* as implanted by the Creator, his own experience of it as uncontrollable passion led him to pronounce it, in the fallen state in which we know it, an *evil*, only to be converted into good when treated not as an end, for the pleasure it gives, but as the means of procreation. (Burnaby, 1967, p. 23)

For Augustine, original sin was itself transmitted by the 'concupiscence' (immoderate desire) of sex. This view was soon welded onto the early Church's celebration of virginity and celibacy, compounding a negative appraisal of sexuality. The Protestant Reformers rejected the medieval idealisation of celibacy, reaffirming a more Jewish emphasis on the duty of marriage and procreation.

Traditionally, sex is only permissible within the institution of marriage. Although some Christian authorities add the further condition 'only for the purpose of procreation', most now recognise the role of sex in giving pleasure, and forging and expressing loving relationships, quite apart from its reproductive function (which is now frequently controlled by contraception). Some liberal Christians argue that sex is morally permissible wherever there is mutual, voluntary, 'informed consent' and an absence of any sort of exploitation (treating the other person not just as a means to one's own gratification), and where it is determined by the fundamental Christian view 'that human relationships should be based on love' (Moore, 1998, p. 229). On this account, which is opposed by more traditional Christians, where there is a contract between equals sex may be allowed even outside marriage.

Divorce and remarriage

Christian debate over divorce may be traced back into the New Testament itself.

EXERCISE
📖 **Read Mark 10:2–12; Matthew 5:31–32 and 19:3–12.**

What similarities and differences may be found between these accounts of Jesus' teaching?

Jesus' own view probably expressed a rejection of the permission for husbands (only) to divorce if they dislike their wives (Deuteronomy 24:1–4) and an elevation of the role of women. But Matthew gives a more qualified version of Jesus' teaching compared with Mark, adding the clause 'except for unchastity' (Matthew 19:9; cf. 5:32). Paul, writing before either evangelist, allows divorce in the case of an 'unbelieving partner' who wishes it (1 Corinthians 7:12–16: the so-called 'Pauline privilege').

The claim that divorce and remarriage, although often tragic, should not be condemned by a compassionate Church is supported by the following arguments.

- There is something oddly partial about the concern that Jesus' teaching on divorce and remarriage should form part of ecclesiastical – and perhaps secular – legislation, while Christians routinely treat so much of Jesus' other teaching as hyperbole or unrealisable ideal (cf. Matthew 5:27–30, 34–37, 39–42). Here, as elsewhere, 'why do we strain at the gnat of sexuality while swallowing camels laden with riches?' (Holloway, 1999, p. 55). Should we not see all Jesus' teaching as part of his *Gospel*, rather than isolating part of it as an attempt to legislate for future generations (cf. Oppenheimer, 1962, pp. 72–74)?
- While a second marriage involves making vows that break one's vows to the first partner, it may be argued that many marriage vows (especially those to love, comfort and honour) *cannot* be fulfilled when the first marriage has broken down. 'Forsaking all others' may be viewed as a promise made in order to love, comfort and honour.
- Marriages are relationships as well as contracts. The traditional understanding of the indissolubility of the marriage bond, forged by God on the basis of life vows freely given by the two partners, witnesses to the seriousness of those promises and of that bond. Yet the personal relationship of the couple sometimes does 'die', 'collapse' or 'dissolve', or is wilfully and deliberately 'broken'.

The Church of England report, *Marriage and the Church's Task*, describes the marriage bond as being created through the partners' ongoing relationship. Tragically, the authors write, it does not always develop a strength such that 'nothing can dissolve' it. 'It is only too possible for men and women to break the bond which God, in principle and in general, wills to be unbreakable, and to put asunder what God, in his original purpose, has joined together' (General Synod Marriage Commission, 1978, p. 38). On this view, when the bond has broken down irretrievably the marriage no longer exists and the partners should be free to seek other relationships. The Roman Catholic Church, however, continues to affirm the indissolubility of the marriage bond (at least of baptised persons), although remarriage after divorce is possible in situations where a marriage has been 'annulled' by the Church (recognised as not being a valid marriage – usually because of some perceived defect in the original decision to marry).

Much of the debate about divorce expresses the fear that the practice is now too common and has extended to situations where it cannot be justified. In the last 25 years the percentage of all families with dependent children in Britain that are headed by separated, divorced or single lone mothers has increased from less than 5% to 19%. The total births 'outside marriage' is now over a third of all live births, although over half of these are joint registrations from the same address (Morgan, 1999, pp. 41–42). Groups or 'family structures' other than the traditional nuclear family have a strong claim to non-discriminatory social and political treatment. But many argue that more should be done to support and strengthen the traditional family on social as well as moral grounds, since research shows that an intact marriage tends to make a positive difference to a dependent child's well-being (Davies, 1993, 1996; David, 1998).

Homosexuality

The Bible forbids adultery, fornication and homosexual acts alike (see, for example, Leviticus 18:20–23; 20:10–16; Deuteronomy 22:13–22; 1 Corinthians 6:9–11). Nevertheless, Christians now routinely ignore not only biblical laws of a ritual or cultic nature, but also many of the laws about property, money, agriculture and sometimes sex (for example Leviticus 15:16–33; Deuteronomy 22:13–28). Christians must therefore choose whether to accept Paul's views on same sex relations in Romans 1, in the same way that they have to decide whether to endorse his argument in Romans 13 that worldly rulers get their authority from God (cf. Holloway, 1999, p. 84). The evangelical Michael Vasey used to remind people that although all the texts about dogs in the Bible are negative, Christians do not regard themselves as bound to adopt a similar attitude to their pets today. The decriminalisation in 1968 of homosexual acts between consenting adults in English law was influenced by pressure from some of the Churches, particularly the Church of England.

EXERCISE

Is homosexuality wrong? What reasons would you give for your response? Would you make a distinction between homosexual 'practice' and 'orientation'?

Find someone who takes a different view from your own. What arguments do they use to support their position?

The crux of the issue is often taken to be that homosexual orientation is 'natural', in the sense that it is an unavoidable part of the genetic, hormonal and psychological make-up of some individuals. There is considerable evidence for this view. Homosexuals may argue, therefore, that 'God has made us like this.' What is more controversial is the claim that they therefore ought not to be denied, or made to feel guilty about, the expression of that God-given nature for their personal fulfilment, especially through the creation of a happy, loving, long-term relationship with a partner of the same sex. Celibacy may still be chosen, by homosexuals as well as heterosexuals, for a higher purpose; but should it be *compulsory* for people of one particular sexual orientation?

In natural law theory homosexual sex is normally condemned as failing to fulfil the proper purpose of sex, which is the procreation of children. But a number of other sexual activities are 'unnatural' on this count, including masturbation and oral sex (which conservative moral preachers still oppose), sex using artificial contraception (which traditional Catholics oppose) and even intercourse when the woman is past the menopause (which surely no one criticises).

Conceptions of contraception

The history of declarations at the ten-yearly Lambeth Conference of bishops of the Anglican Communion traces the changing views within that Church on contraception. In 1908 the bishops declared that Christian people should 'discountenance the use of all artificial means of restriction [of the family] as demoralising to character and hostile to national welfare'. By 1930 they had agreed (with much dissent) that artificial methods of contraception might be used where there were morally sound reasons against abstinence, as well as 'a clearly felt moral obligation to limit or avoid parenthood'. However, complete abstinence was still regarded as 'the primary and obvious method'. By 1958, however, parents were told that they should conscientiously decide if and how they controlled the size of their families, 'in such ways as are acceptable to husband and wife' (Christian Education Movement, 1995, pp. 23–24).

This is only one example of the way in which moral insights grow, and moral fashions change, as the Churches try to come to terms with rapidly changing moral attitudes and behaviour patterns in society. In the case of contraception, the technology – particularly the development of the contraceptive pill for women – has had a more profound effect than any ecclesiastical pronouncement.

The Catholic critique

The traditional view is a version of the natural law argument, in which the natural link between intercourse and conception provides the reason for forbidding *artificial* contraception. Pope Paul VI wrote in his 1968 encyclical, *Humanae Vitae* (§ 13):

> An act of mutual love which impairs the capacity to transmit life which God the Creator, through specific laws, has built into it, frustrates his design which constitutes the norms of marriage, and contradicts the will of the Author of life.

As the 'natural end' (created purpose) of sex is conception, human beings should allow no artificial barriers between the two processes, availing themselves solely of the opportunities provided by the natural cycle of ovulation to have sex with a lower risk of conception (the so-called 'safe period' or 'rhythm method').

However, Thomas Aquinas also recognised that God made human nature in such a way as to promote human happiness. 'What is natural' may then be taken to mean 'what promotes well-being and happiness' (Moore, 1998, p. 236). This insight, coupled with the view that in a proper context of love sex can serve as a form of communication between people, may lead Christians to view many aspects of sexual relationships rather differently.

A female ethic?

The word 'sex' is used both of sexual instincts, desires and behaviour ('having sex') and of the state of being male or female (now often labelled as 'gender'). Over recent decades there has been considerable interest in 'female' and 'feminist' perspectives in both theology and ethics, which often criticise traditional accounts for not having sufficiently 'taken women into account'.

Gilligan's research

Try your hand at the famous 'Heinz' Dilemma', used by Lawrence Kohlberg in his studies of moral thinking (Kohlberg, 1981, p. 12).

Dilemma: Heinz and the stolen drug	Heinz' wife is dying but can be saved by a new drug which is only available from one source, at ten times the cost of manufacture. The druggist refuses to sell the drug to Heinz for less, although Heinz has borrowed half the asking price and promises to pay the rest later. Should Heinz have stolen the drug?

> **EXERCISE**
>
> First consider your own response to this question.
>
> Next, reflect whether males and females would be likely to react differently to this dilemma and indeed to other moral dilemmas.

In Carol Gilligan's research, an 11-year-old boy called Jake responded in a way that was regarded as quite sophisticated on Kohlberg's stage theory of moral development (see Chapter 9 below). He appealed to moral principles rather than personal relationships, claiming that 'a human life is worth more than money'. Amy was an equally bright girl of the same age. Her responses were identified as showing a lower level of moral reasoning, where right was defined in terms of the duties and responsibilities that go with a person's relationships with others. Amy advocated further discussion between Heinz and the druggist: 'I think there might be other ways besides stealing it.' She also refused entirely to reject the druggist's point of view.

According to Gilligan, hers was a typically female reaction that focused on relationships and the effects of different actions on them, whereas the boy favoured logical deduction and a discussion of abstract principles (Gilligan, 1982, pp. 25–32).

Whereas males are often happy to abstract out the 'morally relevant features of a situation' and to make hypothetical decisions about principles 'at a distance', females frequently resist this approach. They are more likely to ask about the precise nature of the relationships within the story. Female ethics are more situational and contextual and less 'universalisable' (see Chapter 1). In Gilligan's view, Kohlberg's research on moral development is flawed partly because it does not take account of the way females think about ethics (but contrast Kohlberg, Levine and Hewer, 1983, pp. 121–150).

The carers?

Such accounts have led to a plea for an ethics that is not so dominated by the ideal of an autonomous (self-governing), rational and independent agent. Room must be found, it is argued, for a female or feminine ethic that is more suitable for the *interdependent* person situated in a network of social relationships. Where males more readily embrace an impartial and impersonal, abstract ethic of justice or duty, females are more concerned with an ethic of (partial and particular) concrete responsibilities and an ethic of care.

EXERCISE

As a male or a female, do you find that your own experience of making moral decisions, including your reflections on the moral dilemmas in this book, gives any support to this view? Find out what others think.

It is surely of moral significance that in most countries a large majority of anti-social and violent people are male. Further, the history and culture of many societies have been shaped by areas of activity which men have dominated and where violence, power and the threat of destruction have been potent forces: from armed conflict down to aggressive economic, political and managerial behaviour. Perhaps there is a particular 'female voice' in morality that stands in marked contrast to all this?

It is often said that the same character traits tend to be praised in women but regarded as faults in men, and vice versa. However, the existence of specifically 'female virtues' has been denied by some feminists as undermining women's dignity (for Rousseau and Ruskin these virtues included dependence, subordination and selflessness). Historically, the idealisation of women has often gone along with a devaluing of their nature, roles and activities. The claim that we each have stereotypically 'feminine' and 'masculine' sides to our nature, whatever our biological sex, may suggest that more 'feminine' men may also have a different 'ethical voice' from more macho members of their own sex.

One fruitful way of thinking about a female ethic is to identify specifically female (or 'feminine') concerns, priorities, conceptions of virtue and value judgements that arise in social practices such as mothering or caring for others. Such a specifically female vision of the good life may 'provide a corrective to the more destructive values and priorities of those spheres of activity which have been dominated by men' (Grimshaw, 1993, p. 494).

Whether or not women reason differently about moral issues, their *ethical priorities* may be different from those of men, perhaps because their life experiences are often different. Men tend to be keener on problem-solving and justifying themselves (and therefore their decisions and actions) whereas women, having evolved as the primary carers who invested heavily in the child and needed to keep the male close, are more concerned to maintain relationships. Therefore women tend towards a mutual, *social*-realisation, often necessitating self-sacrifice, rather than the competitive *self*-realisation of the isolated individual.

This feminine perspective in ethics may run counter to the key ethical notion of 'treating everyone alike'. But we have already noted that in personal relationships everyone is not alike, nor are most of our relationships driven by obligation and 'doing one's duty' – but rather by love, affection and the recognition of the bonds of family and friendship. These are central themes in virtue ethics. Nevertheless, those who are sympathetic to a different, female style in ethics should acknowledge that it needs to be complemented by an appeal to principles, impersonal duty and the calculation of consequences, at least outside the realm of private life.

Further reading

Introductory

Atkinson, D (1994), *Pastoral Ethics*, London, Lynx, part one.

General Synod Board for Social Responsibility (1995), *Something to Celebrate: valuing families in Church and society*, London, Church House Publishing.

General Synod Marriage Commission (1978), *Marriage and the Church's Task*, London, Church Information Office.

Dominian, J (1977), *Proposals for a New Sexual Ethic*, London, Darton, Longman and Todd.

Grenz, S (1998), *Sexual Ethics: a biblical perspective*, Carlisle, Paternoster.

Holloway, R (1999), *Godless Morality: keeping religion out of ethics*, Edinburgh, Canongate, chapters 2 and 3.

House of Bishops of the General Synod (1991), *Issues in Human Sexuality*, London, Church House Publishing.

Vardy, P (1997), *The Puzzle of Sex*, London, HarperCollins.

Vasey, M (1995), *Strangers and Friends: a new exploration of homosexuality and the Bible*, London, Hodder and Stoughton.

Advanced

Atkinson, R (1965), *Sexual Morality*, London, Hutchinson.

Barton, S C (ed.) (1996), *The Family in Theological Perspective*, Edinburgh, T and T Clark.

Cahill, L S (1996), *Sex, Gender and Christian Ethics*, Cambridge, Cambridge University Press.

Gilligan, C (1982), *In a Different Voice: psychological theory and women's development*, Cambridge, Massachusetts, Harvard University Press.

Parsons, S F (1996), *Feminism and Christian Ethics*, Cambridge, Cambridge University Press.

Thatcher, A (1993), *Liberating Sex: a Christian sexual theology*, London, SPCK.

Thatcher, A (1999), *Marriage after Modernity: Christian marriage in postmodern times*, Sheffield, Sheffield Academic Press.

6. WEALTH AND WORK

Introduction

Even those who claim to be above such things, or who have little enough of either of them, find their lives moulded by the power of wealth and work.

Reflecting on experience

What moral issues concern you about:

- the amount of your income and wealth (savings, possessions);
- your future financial prospects;
- the amount of your charitable giving?

Work

'Anyone unwilling to work should not eat', Paul writes. The first Christians were exhorted to follow the model of the apostles themselves ('with toil and labour we worked night and day, so that we might not burden any one of you'), to eschew idleness and 'to do their work quietly and to earn their own living' (2 Thessalonians 3:7–12). Here Paul is firmly rooted in Jewish tradition. Like God the creator, the Israelites are commanded to labour six days before their sabbath rest (Exodus 20:9), although Jesus does the work of God even on the sabbath – for 'my Father is still working' (John 5:17; cf. Luke 13:14–17).

Although the story in Genesis 3 suggests that work (or at least gardening!) only becomes toil and sweated labour because of God's curse on the ground (v. 17), work of some sort is a biological necessity for humans. Perhaps for that reason, it is a sort of psychological necessity also. Sigmund Freud remarked that 'all that matters is love and work.' The two are similar in some ways, as both are a form of self-giving, with a focus outside their originator, which can bring order and value out of chaos and disvalue. Often we are more satisfied at work than at leisure, unless our leisure also becomes a sort of work.

The rewards and punishment of work

If work is not satisfying, there is always pay day. Not 'always', of course: the work of the student, the mother and the volunteer is unpaid, and much work is poorly paid. Workplaces also vary, with whole industries depending on working conditions that most of us would find impossible to endure, physically or mentally.

EXERCISE
A 'just reward' is the reward a person deserves; justice is getting one's 'deserts'. Before reading further, jot down the criteria that you think ought to determine how much people are paid.

This question may sound rather quaint and old-fashioned, for we have largely ceased to expect any moral dimension to operate in this area. Nevertheless, John Hospers presents a useful classification of the criteria of distributive justice that have been cited in discussions about pay (Hospers, 1972, chapter 19). The first two of these are different ways of quantifying the work done.

1. **Achievement** is what is actually accomplished by our work. This criterion for reward operates in exams or 'piece work' in factories. But how do we compare different sorts of achievements (teachers against doctors, for example)?

2. **Effort** is another sense of the word 'work', focusing on the time and energy expended in doing work. As young children we were sometimes rewarded for effort rather than achievement, but should dull but hard-working students or employees be rewarded more than the bright ones who finish the job or the exam in half the time?

3. **Ability** may mean our native ability (which is outside our control) or our acquired skills (which are partly the result of effort). In any case, why should an employer reward mere ability, rather than its products?

4. **Need** is a controversial criterion. 'Rewarding in proportion to need would be rewarding the spendthrift and ne'er-do-well and penalizing the person who works hardest and tries most valiantly to prevent himself from becoming needy in the future' (Hospers, 1972, p. 368).

These first four criteria relate to the workers and the product of their work; criteria 5 to 7 relate more to society.

5. **The 'open market'** is in practice the key determinant of the wages of many people in 'free economies', through the laws of supply and demand. It is, we are often told, impossible to 'buck the market' and workers must not 'price themselves out of the market'. In a real market the stall that charges less for good quality bananas will sell out first. But is this a criterion of *justice*? Do teachers and nurses *deserve* less than footballers and pop stars? Most of us cannot simply change jobs as the demand for labour changes and most of us are unqualified to do many other jobs (cauliflowers cannot change into bananas just because bananas are selling well today).

6. **Public need** for the work that we do is another possible criterion for a 'just reward'. But need is a relative term: is your work needed for human survival or enjoyment? How do we *measure* need: by its urgency, the extent to which it is shared, or what?

7. **Public desire** for the product of our labour is a consideration that brings us close to criterion 5 again, for markets are in the hands of customers with their consumer desires. But again, is it a matter of desert and justice that the pop star can earn more than the firefighter?

8. **Other criteria** include the long training required for many trades and professions, the financial and physical risk of some forms of employment, and the unpleasant or taxing nature of many jobs. Should pay reflect these factors, not only because no one would do the job otherwise, but also as a consideration of *justice*?

Utilitarians argue that these criteria are themselves justified because applying them tends to increase the general happiness. On this view, *justice* is a part of *utility*. Others disagree: 'What a person deserves depends not on what will occur in the future as a result of his actions but on what he has done in the past' – his effort and qualifications, or his dangerous work-situation (Hospers, 1972, p. 373).

Freedom

Understood as the absence of external constraint, rather than as a philosophical claim about our 'free will', the urge for human freedom has found expression in three areas of great concern for social ethics. All three freedoms are *limited* freedoms, of course, and the freedom of one individual must be balanced against the rights and freedom of others.

- **Political freedom** allows individuals to meet and form interest groups and political parties ('freedom of assembly'); it forbids slavery or unjust imprisonment. Some form of democracy is usually regarded as an essential part of political freedom, together with other 'civil freedoms' such as equality before the law, freedom of speech and freedom to engage in public worship.
- **Social freedom** complements political freedom. It includes 'freedom to be educated', 'freedom to work', 'freedom from poverty' and 'freedom from discrimination'.
- **Economic freedom** is the freedom to acquire and hold private property. Right-wing politicians and social thinkers often argue for the advance of economic freedoms at the expense of social freedoms; those on the left take the opposite view. Classical socialism restricts the economic freedom of (most) individuals through public ownership, arguing that this enhances social freedom by allowing everyone 'freedom of access' to property and the pooled fruits of the labour of individuals.

Economic justice

Central to the ideal of justice are the notions of 'equal treatment' and 'just distribution'. Debate in social ethics has converged on what is involved in distributive justice and the extent to which a just distribution should be based on prior rights to possessions, agreed contracts for the exchange of wealth, the need or role of the recipients, or the overall good of society.

Robert Nozick underscores the significance of economic freedom in arguing against State intervention in redistributing wealth. He favours instead the *commutative justice* of voluntary exchanges among individuals all of whom have a natural right to their own wealth (Nozick, 1974, chapter 7). States should not intervene in such transactions; indeed they should exercise no more than a minimal role, avoiding taxation (viewed here as the coercive taking of wealth) as far as possible.

By contrast, John Rawls' interpretation of justice involves a long-term redistribution to the benefit of the poor and disadvantaged (Rawls, 1972). His rather Kantian 'social contract' perspective (see Chapter 2) rejects utilitarian thinking in favour of shared rights. It may be seen as a generalisation of the golden rule, which itself is part of the moral viewpoint of treating people equally.

Nozick and Rawls begin with the individual and follow an abstract, rational approach to ethics. Their viewpoints are often referred to as broadly *liberal* accounts. By contrast, *communitarians* reject these emphases and regard notions of justice as emerging in the practices of particular communities and traditions.

EXERCISE

Look up the nouns 'justice' and 'righteousness' (and related terms if you have time) in a Bible concordance. Follow up some of the references you find there.

Biblical notions of justice reflect God's concern for the rights and welfare of the poor and oppressed. The God of the prophets demands that injustice be overthrown and redressed. Recent Christian social ethics, drawing on liberation theology, has spoken similarly of a 'preferential option to the poor' and of the poor as 'the litmus test of justice', arguing that justice must be measured by their plight and by their knowledge of what justice requires, rather than the claims of the rich (Lebacqz, 1998, p. 168).

Equality

This is a key concept in the moral point of view, whether expressed in the language of equality of worth, equal rights or impartiality in decision-making. In the political and economic fields, however, debate has centred on two more problematic areas.

Equality of opportunity is the principle that individuals should all have the same chances to acquire whatever qualifications are needed for different positions (university entrance, for example, or paid employment), coupled with the principle that those positions be awarded solely on the basis of those qualifications. 'Qualifications' is a wide term and may cover examination grades, abilities, knowledge or experience.

Although widely applauded, this principle is violated by societies that treat people differently ('discriminate') because of their social or ethnic background, colour, gender, age, wealth or disability.

Equality of income or wealth is sometimes endorsed as an ideal. In principle, communist societies are places where wealth is vested in the State and individuals work for the common good, each contributing 'according to his capacity' and receiving payment 'according to his need'. Outside such a context, economic equality reduces to equality of opportunity coupled with some redistribution of wealth from richer to poorer members of society.

Very often the debate over equality is about the extent to which any such redistribution of wealth is justified. Even *market liberals* such as Friedrich Hayek and Milton Friedman may argue for minimum levels of income, through a form of negative income tax. But they are opposed to using 'progressive taxation' (in which the tax rate increases with the income or capital sum being taxed) to fund welfare or aid programmes, viewing this as 'social engineering' and an unjustified curb on personal liberty (presumably of the rich). They argue that the market that is created by voluntary transactions between free individuals (over employment, investment and purchasing goods and services) should suffice, except for the poorest in society. *Liberal democrats*, however, favour more redistribution of wealth than the markets allow. They also tend to be more concerned with the injustice of the relative disparity between rich and poor, rather than limiting their concern to situations of absolute poverty.

Should Christians be communists?

EXERCISE

Your local Church or student Christian group is hosting a debate on this question. Four churchgoers have been invited to speak: a Conservative MP, the owner of a local family firm, a radical left-wing socialist and a member of a religious community (who has taken a vow of poverty). You have been asked to research 'the Bible's view' on the question. The chairman has suggested that you might discuss some of the following texts: Leviticus 25; Deuteronomy 15; Matthew 6:19–34 and 19:16–30; Luke 16; Acts 2:44–47 and 5:1–11; 2 Thessalonians 3:6–13 and 2 Corinthians 9. ▶▶

> What main points would you make and how might the others
> respond to these points?

The Old Testament view is that 'the earth is the Lord's and all that is
in it' and humans are not the owners but the stewards of creation
(Psalm 24:1; Genesis 1 and 2). Jewish law is full of provisions to protect
the poor and the debtor, and to restrict the avarice of property-owners
and kings. Jesus speaks strong words against those who rely on material riches. He seems to have himself adopted the role of an itinerant
preacher and teacher of wisdom, dependent on others (unlike Paul) for
food and shelter. The first Christian community in Jerusalem dispensed
with private property altogether, owning all things in common.

The fourth-century bishop John Chrysostom is typical of the early
fathers in the line he takes on private property:

> 'Mine' and 'thine' – those chilly words which introduce innumerable
> wars into the world – should be eliminated from the Church . . . The
> poor would not envy the rich, because there would be no rich . . . All
> things would be in common. (Quoted in Gorringe, 1998, p. 176)

Thomas Aquinas is less forthright yet even he recognises no absolute
rights to ownership. Private property is conducive to peace but when
others are in extreme need they have a right to it; the rich man sins 'if
he unreasonably prevents others from using it' (*Summa Theologiae*,
2a2ae, 66, 2; Vol. 38, 1975, p. 69).

However, the rise of trade and commerce and thus of the 'market
economy' was soon to lead to a new justification of private ownership.
John Locke held that the purpose of society is to preserve property
rights; these rights derive ultimately from a person's right to his own
body and its labour (Locke, Book II, Chapter V, § 27). Locke's views
were challenged by Jean-Jacques Rousseau, who famously asserted that
'the fruits of the earth belong to us all, and the earth itself to nobody'
(Rousseau, 1754, second part), and even more famously by Karl Marx,
who argued for a society where there was common ownership of the
means of production (Marx, 1875, I). The French social reformer,
Pierre-Joseph Proudhon, declared in 1840 that 'property is theft'.

Timothy Gorringe has argued that the ecological facts of global life
demand a change in our attitude to property. He proposes four principles derived from pre-capitalist wisdom (Gorringe, 1998, pp. 182–184):

- the acknowledgement 'of all that we have as gift';
- the case 'for every human community to have access to the goods of the earth' (which will only be possible as we 'live simply that others may simply live');
- the principle that our property, privacy and freedom can only be had in relationships of interdependence and should not be had at the expense of others (our supposed right 'to do what *I* want when I want how I want [is] a pathetic fixation at psychological age three'!);
- the need to put property in its place (as did Jesus), lest we be bound by the chains of Mammon, consumption and the market place.

EXERCISE
Review Gorringe's four principles. What is your view of them and why?

Global warning

The disparity between rich and poor in world terms is as well-known as it is startling. The statistics reveal a growing proportion of global income, currently over 80%, going to the richest 20% of the world's population; whereas a declining proportion, currently less than 1.5%, is shared by the poorest 20%. This poorest one fifth, comprising one thousand million human beings, live in absolute poverty and insecurity, subject to disease, drought and starvation that shortens their life, inflicts great suffering and robs them of human dignity. Ecological and political pressures, as well as the demands of morality, seem to call for a redistribution of wealth on a global scale. Yet this is greeted with suspicion by many. Archbishop Helder Camara remarked, 'When I help the poor I am called a saint, but when I ask why they are poor I am called a communist.'

The causes of world poverty include the incompetence and corruption of some leaders, and tribal, ethnic, religious and civil wars. But there is no doubt that international trade and economic activity can sometimes exploit the poor for the sake of profits for rich nations and companies.

The very size of the problem suggests that 'there is a special moral urgency or seriousness attached to absolute poverty', writes Nigel Dower. 'Should we say: the more evil something is, the greater moral reason there is, other things being equal, to reduce it?' (Dower, 1993, p. 277).

EXERCISE

Claims about our duty to alleviate world poverty are often resisted by the assertion that our duties relate to our immediate society or 'moral community'. How would utilitarians, deontologists and those who advocate virtue ethics respond to this insistence that charity should begin and end at home? How do you respond to it?

The objection is based on the idea of morality as arising in, and therefore being limited to, a particular moral community, with its agreed bonds of mutual interaction and co-operation. Even the Bible can limit love and justice to the community of Israel or the (sometimes very local) early Church (cf. 2 John 9–11), as well as recognising that morality must transcend the local (cf. Leviticus 19:33–34; Matthew 5:43–48).

Although we may have specific responsibilities to those with whom we have close relationships or have made commitments, there does not seem to be a valid argument for *limiting* our duty of care to such people. In any case, you might want to argue that the world itself should now be seen as a moral community, on account of the global inter-actions and economic inter-dependencies in which we are already engaged.

But *how much* ought we to care? Many Christian saints, known and unknown, have thought that we should sacrifice ourselves for the needs of the world. Dower suggests a more qualified caring: 'we ought to care for others as much as we can consistent with a reasonable concern for the quality of our own lives' (Dower, 1993, p. 282). This, he says, will still constitute a challenge for most of us.

What do you think?

Business ethics: a contradiction in terms?

At the heart of much criticism of economic and commercial activity is the claim that people are being treated not as persons, of value as ends in themselves, but as means to non-personal, financial ends – as things or commodities. A concern for the market-place is central to business thinking, quite naturally. It is as absurd as it is counterproductive to criticise business for taking the market seriously, unless we propose dismantling capitalism and curbing economic freedom. Nevertheless, the market can be a rough old place and many would wish to argue for some sort of *qualification* of both the rhetoric and the practice of market economics.

First, it has been denied that there is something entirely 'natural' about wholesale competition and selfishness; rather it is particular social conditions that develop these characteristics.

Second, the free market is said to cheapen human relationships by ignoring issues of moral merit and intrinsic value, assessing everything and everyone solely in terms of 'price', 'profit' and what may be bought and sold (cf. Scruton, 1999, pp. 30, 84).

Third, there is a point to be made about the nature of Christian values:

> The list of virtues associated with [the] distinctively Christian form of life do not include 'enterprise' and 'entrepreneurship' – which is not to say that they are wrong, only that they have not the place in the quality of life worth living which many others would attribute to them. (Pring, 1996, p. 68)

Defenders of the market may resist criticisms of this sort, arguing that a *just* society is precisely one in which people are free to pursue their own ends without interference or that virtue can be promoted by business.

EXERCISE
In a business context, do moral virtues become mere second-order principles which may – and ought? – to be overridden by the first-order principles of production, consumption and profit?

Note that profit is not the only purpose of business. Its primary objective is to provide certain services or manufacture certain goods. Creating profit and providing employment may be seen as proper secondary objectives: good ends in themselves which also support the primary objective. But in fact a business may have many objectives and many responsibilities: to its customers, its workforce, the environment, its local community and society as a whole, in addition to its responsibilities to the shareholders who ultimately 'own' it.

According to Robert Solomon, a business corporation should 'serve the public' rather than itself alone (Solomon, 1993, p. 361). He criticises the rather overblown rhetoric about the role of competition in business.

> However competitive a particular industry may be, it always rests on a foundation of shared interests and mutually agreed-upon rules of conduct, and the competition takes place not in a jungle but in a community which it presumably both serves and depends upon. Business life is first of all fundamentally co-operative. It is only within the bounds of mutually shared concerns that competition is possible. (Solomon, 1993, p. 358)

This argument may be further developed. Business and markets are themselves often sustained by a sub-structure of comparatively lowly paid workers without which no business would exist and no profits would be possible. Beyond them lies the whole fabric of our society, which rests on the *wholly unpaid* devotion, love and service of human relationships.

> I am thinking here particularly of parents, but also of the informal networks of human support and care (and 'production') that are provided by relatives, neighbours and friends ... While we need to recognise that public services are parasitic on the 'business community', let us also acknowledge that those businesses are themselves parasitic on the 'private services' of a real community: a community that they did not create, do not pay for and have no moral right to control ... Markets are not the only 'forces' that exist. They are just the easiest places in which to negotiate a price. Some expenditures of energy, though costly, are not bought and sold there. And others cannot be, for they would be dissipated in the transaction. Love can have no price. (Astley, 1998, p. 383)

While we should not ignore the positive value of self-reliance, independent responsibility and other virtues that a culture of competitiveness can bring (Higginson, 1997), Christians may join with others in condemning the *unqualified* endorsement of profit and competition that lies behind some of the assumptions of the market-place. People must come first.

Further reading

Introductory

Higginson, R (1997), *The Ethics of Business Competition: the law of the jungle?*, Cambridge, Grove Books.

Sider, R J (1997), *Rich Christians in an Age of Hunger*, London, Hodder and Stoughton.

Vardy, P (1989), *Business Morality: people and profit*, London, Marshall Pickering.

Advanced

Dower, N (1998), *World Ethics: the new agenda*, Edinburgh, Edinburgh University Press.

Gorringe, T J (1994), *Capital and the Kingdom: theological ethics and economic order*, London, SPCK.

Honderich, T (1991), *Conservatism*, Harmondsworth, Penguin.

Preston, R H (1987), *The Future of Christian Ethics*, London, SCM.

Sedgwick, P H (1999), *The Market Economy and Christian Ethics*, Cambridge University Press.

Selby, P (1997), *Grace and Mortgage: the language of faith and the debt of the world*, London, Darton, Longman and Todd.

Tawney, R H (1926), *Religion and the Rise of Capitalism*, London, John Murray.

Wogaman, J P (1986), *Economics and Ethics: a Christian enquiry*, London, SCM.

7. WAR AND PUNISHMENT

Introduction

We are concerned here with political and social questions about how a State should behave to its own citizens and to those of other nations. Obviously, decisions on these issues impact on individuals. It is individuals who suffer and die in wars, and it is individuals who lose their liberty – and in some places their life – through judicial punishment.

Reflecting on experience
You will probably not have suffered yourself as a prisoner or victim of war. But through print and TV journalism, films and literature we have all been able to empathise with those who undergo such experiences. Reflecting on such situations ask yourself, 'Under what circumstances can I justify the suffering that has been inflicted on these people?'

Justified war?

It is often said that war is a special case. During the miners' strikes of the early 1970s a senior trades unionist, a Christian, was invited to write a piece for a religious magazine on the morality of strikes. He refused, saying: 'There is no morality of strikes. A strike is a state of war.'

The effects of war on the attitudes of society has been as devastating as its effects on the landscape and economies of nations. The optimism and triumphalist nationalism of the European nations was shattered by years of seemingly pointless slaughter during the First World War. Belief in the intrinsic decency of modern, civilised States was shaken by the atrocities committed during the Second World War. And what of the effects of the apparent suspension, even reversal, of morality?

In close combat the moral resources of those fighting may be eroded and at times overwhelmed. The human responses may be eroded by a culture of combat in which opponents are humiliated or dehumanized, or by soldiers developing a defensive hardness. Moral identity may be neutralized by training or by the remote and alien context of the battlefield. Additional weakening may come from the contempt for scruples expressed within the culture of combat: 'It's a tough war, Chaplain.' (Glover, 1999, p. 113)

During a war, that which was previously condemned is now considered obligatory, and private concerns and rights are routinely overridden. Yet one moral philosopher writes that 'apart from important side-effects, killing in war is morally on a par with other killing. Declarations of war, military uniforms and solemn utterances by national leaders in no way reduce the burden of justification for an act of killing' (Glover, 1977, p. 252).

EXERCISE

Where do you stand on the morality of war? What do you take to be the Christian view on this issue?

Do you believe that deliberate killing by a soldier in wartime is morally different from murder?

I consider here three views on the justification of war.

Political realism

This is the claim that moral norms do not apply to war because they apply only to individuals and it is States that go to war. Furthermore, States should only be concerned with their national interest: with what is 'prudent' for them rather than what is 'morally right'. Those who give States or causes *unlimited rights* to protect or promote their collective interests, unlike the limited rights we each have as individual members of a State, draw close to this position, especially if they ignore the interests of other States or groups.

Pacifism

'Absolute pacifists', by contrast, argue that war (or any violence) can never be justified. People who believe strongly in the sanctity of human

life, or of each individual's right to life, are likely to hold this unequivo-
cal position. It is often assumed that it is the only consistent Christian
view.

EXERCISE
Try to list elements in the stories about Jesus that reveal his attitude
to violence. If you can, find the relevant biblical references with the
help of a concordance. Was Jesus a pacifist?

Jesus' ministry was exercised within a country that was under the
occupation of a foreign power. Forty years after his execution by that
power, the Jews rebelled against the Romans. Their capital and temple
were destroyed and most of the Jewish survivors were expelled from
their Promised Land. This is the context of such 'pacifist' texts as
Matthew 5:38–48. Additionally, Jesus saw his own death as necessary to
God's plan and for that reason did not resist it (see Mark 14:21 and
32–36; Matthew 26:51–54).

Pacifism in its absolute form proposes that *nothing* could ever justify
war or violence, even in self-defence. But if we have a right to prevent
the evil of violence befalling us, and if that right extends to violent self-
defence, then pacifism is impossible. Most moral theories recognise situations in which such defensive responses appear to be justified.

The term 'pacifism' covers the variety of positions that have been
embraced by Christians such as Francis of Assisi, George Fox and the
Quakers, Leo Tolstoy, the Mennonites, Thomas Merton and Martin
Luther King. However, many theologians regard it as an impracticable,
naive and even heretical position, relevant only to individual morality
rather than the relationships between groups. Reinhold Niebuhr argued
that our real nature has often to be contained by coercive power; love is
no substitute for the institutions of justice (Niebuhr, 1932, chapter 7).
In 1940 Karl Barth wrote: 'The Church of Jesus Christ cannot and will
not make war. . . . Yet the Churches must . . . tell every people that it is
necessary and worthwhile to fight and to suffer for just peace' (quoted
in Reeves and Kaye, 1999, p. 53).

A more defensible, *qualified form of pacifism* has been framed in
recognition of the fact that modern war is almost certain to kill
innocent people (the killing of children being the clearest example). If
these innocents have a right to life – and surely they do, in the absence

of special, overriding circumstances – then that killing is a serious evil. Hence:

> the burden, and it is a heavy one, rests upon anyone who would seek to justify behaviour that has as a consequence the death of innocent persons . . . In any major war, none of those considerations that can sometimes justify engaging in war will in fact come close to meeting this burden. (Wasserstrom, 1975b, pp. 330–331)

One consideration that we should bear in mind here, however, is that some aggressive States and regimes have shown themselves willing to inflict quite horrendous suffering on innocent people and even to engage in their ruthless extermination. Does that factor bring us any closer to 'meeting this burden'? If as an armed policeman I am fairly sure that the deranged man threatening the passengers on the school bus will kill them all unless I shoot *now*, you may excuse (on the principle of double effect) the fact that my shot also kills the innocent bus driver standing behind him. Or would you?

The 'just war'

The middle ground between extreme versions of political realism and of pacifism has been occupied by the theory of the just war. Originating as early as the writings of Augustine, the view that war may be justified for the preservation or establishment of a righteous peace was codified by Thomas Aquinas. Thomas argued that for a war to be just it must have:

- a *lawful authority* (no war can be justified if is waged by private individuals);
- a *just cause* ('those who are attacked are attacked because they deserve it on account of some wrong they have done' – *Summa Theologiae*, 2a2ae, 40, 1; Vol. 35, 1972, p. 83); and
- a *right intention* (to defeat the enemy in order to establish peace, not for national expansion or the humiliation of other nations).

Later, a fourth condition was added by de Vitoria, that the war be waged *in a just manner*. This has come to be understood in terms of minimal force exercised against legitimate targets in such a way that the war's bad consequences do not outweigh its expected good results. This condition was cited by Bishop George Bell in 1944 in criticism of the obliteration bombing of German cities by Allied aircraft.

International agreements such as the Hague and Geneva Conventions have laid down rules restricting the use of certain weapons and regulating the treatment of the sick and wounded in times of war.

Although such legislation seems bizarre or futile to many, these rules rest on the conviction that it is *unlimited* war that cannot be justified.

Nuclear war and deterrence

A full-scale nuclear war would seem to breach the just war conditions of how a war should be fought, for the requirements of *discrimination* (that only legitimate targets be killed) and of *proportionality* (that the bad consequences should not exceed the achievable good) hardly hold in a situation of such indiscriminate devastation. As one moral theologian put it, the use of nuclear weapons 'would not be to restrain the enemy from further evil: it would be to destroy them utterly and in that destruction to destroy whatever is good in them and every hope of the triumph of that good' (Bishop John Mortimer, quoted in Wood, 1961, p. 85).

To *threaten* nuclear war in order to deter others involves an intention, under certain circumstances, of waging this sort of war. Many opponents of nuclear weapons argue that, if they are not (risky) political bluffs or 'insincere threats', these intentions are themselves evil because they intend to do something that is so obviously wrong.

EXERCISE

Can a major nuclear strike ever be justified, particularly if it is made *in retaliation* for a nuclear attack that has already largely devastated the victim nation? (You may recall some of the arguments in the film 'Dr Strangelove'.)

Religious pacifism revisited

Stanley Hauerwas is a doughty champion of non-violence, claiming that it is 'at the very heart of our understanding of God' (Hauerwas, 1984, p. xvii). Nevertheless, he recognises the power of the claims (a) that the State should be permitted to use violence to restrain those who do not respect the lives and rights of others, and as a (necessary) means to preserve freedom and justice, and (b) that the Christian may resort to violence so as to create freedom and justice where they are absent. He therefore has some sympathy with the questioner who asks, 'Are Christians not unjust if they allow another person to be injured or even killed if they might prevent that by the use of violence?' Yet he insists:

The problem with these attempts to commit the Christian to limited use of violence is that they too often distort the character of our alternatives. Violence used in the name of justice, or freedom, or equality is seldom simply a matter of justice – it is a matter of the power of some over others. Moreover, when violence is justified in principle as a necessary strategy for securing justice, it stills the imaginative search for nonviolent ways of resistance to injustice. For true justice never comes through violence, nor can it be based on violence. It can only be based on truth, which has no need to resort to violence to secure its own existence. (Hauerwas, 1984, pp. 114–115)

A connection between truth, non-violence and justice was also highlighted by the great Hindu political and spiritual leader Mahatma Gandhi. He held that selfless action precluded violent action (in his view, against *all* living things). Hundreds of his followers were bloodily beaten as they staged a silent demonstration in the famous 'Salt March' of 1930, an example of non-violence that attracted the attention and sympathy of the world to the Indians' claims for independence and was instrumental in achieving peaceful political change. For Gandhi (who believed that 'God is Truth'), non-violence and truth were two sides of the same coin; there was no way to find truth except by means of the way of non-violence.

The Christian theologian Peter Hodgson interprets Ghandi's claim that the pursuit of truth is a 'spiritual force' as an appeal to 'the power of the Spirit, not the power of weapons and wealth' (Hodgson, 1994, p. 311). Others might offer a more psychological interpretation of the effectiveness of non-violence in converting the violent and unjust (although God's Spirit creates and sustains human psychology). However it happens, evil and hatred may sometimes be 'absorbed' and 'neutralised' by one who passively receives them without retaliation. So the mother holding the kicking child takes his blows until they disappear and are turned into hugs. And the behaviour of a Nelson Mandela, in treating his prison guards with respect and kindness over many years, has had an undeniable wider effect.

The Christian will inevitably think here of the one who faced his enemies 'like a sheep that before its shearers is silent' (Isaiah 53:4–12; cf. 1 Peter 2:21–25; Acts 8:32–35), having taught his disciples that a blow to the cheek should be met by offering 'the other also' (Matthew 5:39). At the crucifixion the hatred of the world (including the State and religion) did its best to inflict its mortal wound on Jesus. It succeeded: hatred and violence won. But according to the Christian perception their victory was their defeat. Jesus absorbed and bore 'the sin of the world', nailing it to the cross. 'When the centurion, who stood facing him, saw that in this way he breathed his last, he said, "Truly this man was God's son" ' (Mark 15:39).

Punishment

Like war, punishment seems to go against our moral rule not to cause another person to suffer, in this case by limiting his freedom. Theories of punishment seek to provide a moral basis for this practice.

Dilemma: the prisoners	Two young men have been convicted of identical robberies. Steve is well-educated and seems to come from a 'good home'. Matt never knew his father and at sixteen was thrown out by his mother. He performed poorly at school and is dependent on drugs. He has been in prison before. The judge must sentence them.

> **EXERCISE**
> Do you think the two should receive the same punishment? What reasons could you offer to defend your decision?

Your views on this dilemma might reveal your own perspective on the 'point' of punishment.

Vindication
Punishment may be seen as a symbolic affair, vindicating the 'respect for the law' which is so essential for a healthy, cohesive society. According to Lord Denning, 'the ultimate justification of any punishment . . . is the emphatic denunciation by the community of the crime' (Royal Commission on Capital Punishment, 1953, paragraph 53). This reflects the legitimate 'resentment against vice and wickedness' (Butler, 1726) felt by society against certain sorts of crime. This justification is closely related to the idea of punishment as retribution; the words 'vengeance', 'avenge' and 'revenge' all derive from the Latin word for 'vindicate'.

Retribution

Punishment is justified on this account (as on the last) simply because a crime has been committed. Many claim that the retributive theory is the only one that justifies the punishment of *the person who is actually guilty of the crime*, and that it is the most 'natural view' and the one most likely to provide the victim of crime with a proper sense that justice has been done.

This theory, unlike others, implies that the punishment be proportionate to the crime, as 'appropriate' retribution, requital or vengeance. The Old Testament's law of retaliation (*lex talionis*), the rule of 'eye for eye, tooth for tooth' (Leviticus 24:17–22; Deuteronomy 19:21), might seem to illustrate this position. However, that law appears to have been framed to *limit* retribution so that it did not spiral out of all proportion to the actual offence.

But judicial retribution is an impassive judicial accounting, quite independent of the feelings of hatred and anger that accompany passionate revenge. Rather, at the heart of the retributive theory lies the claim that punishment is justified solely because the offender has voluntarily committed the crime. In this sense wrongdoers *deserve* to suffer for their wrongdoing: they 'brought it on themselves' by breaking the law. On a Kantian view, this would be to treat the criminal as an 'end-in-himself' – a rational, responsible agent of intrinsic worth and dignity. Criminals are not sick patients to be healed, nor are they irresponsible agents like children or animals. Punishment is never to be imposed 'merely as a means to promote some other good for the criminal himself or for civil society . . . [but] only because he has committed a crime' (Kant, 1996, p. 105).

As this penal suffering is regarded as good in itself, quite apart from any good consequences, the theory suits deontologists whereas all the other theories we shall consider are broadly utilitarian justifications (see Chapter 2). The retributive theory looks to the past, endorsing punishment *because of*; utilitarian theories look to the future and approve of punishment only *in order to* (Hospers, 1972, pp. 381–382). According to Jeremy Bentham, all punishment is evil because it hurts people and it can only be justified if its good effects outweigh this evil.

Deterrence

Judges sometimes speak of handing down an 'exemplary sentence' to an offender. The idea here is that the punishment of one criminal can serve to deter others from crime, as well as discouraging the offender himself from re-offending. Justifying punishment on account of its deterrent effect is a popular liberal position, although in the UK three-quarters of those who have served a prison sentence re-offend.

The theory of deterrence may also be criticised on other grounds. One troubling implication is that deterrence 'uses' the offender as a means to the good of others. Another is that the punishment of an *innocent person* can have as strong a deterrent effect on others as the punishment of the guilty.

Dilemma: judicial framing

Suppose that a particularly horrific crime has been committed by a member of one racial or religious group against a member of a different group, and unless an innocent member of the first group is framed for the crime, the people in the second group will take the law into their own hands and attack other innocent members of the first group. Swift punishment is needed . . . but the guilty person cannot be found, whereas it is quite easy to fabricate evidence against an innocent person. (Ten, 1993, p. 367)

EXERCISE
Would framing an innocent person be justifiable in this situation for utilitarian reasons?

Reform

This view focuses more on the needs of the offender and is undergirded by a therapeutic, rather than a punitive, motivation. It thinks of offenders as people who need help, education, and possibly medical treatment, so as to promote a change in their behaviour that will prevent them committing further criminal acts. Advocates will naturally seek to make prison regimes less brutal, degrading and repressive, seeing the role of prison as socialising and humanising (despite the evidence in most cases).

Some may question whether loss of liberty as such can serve as a reformatory influence; indeed one striking implication of the reform theory is that the processes of reform need not be *unpleasant* at all.

Protection

At least prison stops prisoners committing crimes while they are there. As it is a duty of the State to protect its citizens, we may argue that some offenders ought to be imprisoned for the protection of society. In some cases imprisonment also serves as a protection to the offender himself, particularly from revenge attacks from his victims or from other criminals he may have betrayed.

Capital punishment

EXERCISE
📖 **Read Genesis 9:5–6; Numbers 35:9–34.**

Can these biblical injunctions be justified today?

Many Christians would lay more stress on principles such as the sanctity of human life in determining whether the State is morally permitted to execute its citizens. The last executions took place in Britain in 1964. In opposing the death sentence Archbishop Michael Ramsey argued that although retribution was a necessary aspect of punishment, we must strive for 'the possibility of reclamation . . . of a person being alive, repentant, and different'. He also held that the death penalty devalued human life (Potter, 1993, p. 201). The Anglican Church was a relatively late convert to this abolitionist position, by contrast with the long history of principled opposition to capital punishment shown by others, notably the Quakers.

Back in 1785, Archdeacon William Paley had justified hanging on utilitarian grounds rather than as a matter of justice. This conformed with the view of execution as *the* exemplary punishment, a position illustrated by a judge's reprieving one girl for housebreaking but condemning another to death so as to set an example. The latter miscreant was to die 'to enforce a law . . . aimed not at [her] death, but at the death of her crime', according to His Lordship (Potter, 1993, p. 10).

Experience in Britain and elsewhere has indicated that abolition has made little difference to the number of murders, many of which are committed in situations of passionate conflict when thoughts of the risk of a death sentence exercise little influence. This is a strong utilitarian argument against capital punishment. Many countries still practise it, however. Nearly four hundred executions took place in the USA in the 1990s, and at the time of writing some 3,600 prisoners are in American prisons awaiting execution. Those States that do practise this ultimate form of punishment run the risk of executing an innocent person. They also lay themselves open to the charge of psychologically torturing the prisoner (and his innocent relatives), through anticipation of his death. But some would argue that this is little worse than the situation of the terminally-ill (although they will not know the date of their death) or that it is itself a just additional punishment.

Retributivists such as Kant argue that capital punishment is the only appropriate (because the only 'proportionate') punishment for a grave offence such as murder: justice demands a life for a life. Bereaved parents of murdered children are likely to endorse that view and to feel that the utilitarian perspective implicitly regards the life of the victim as of lesser value than the life of the murderer.

Statistics show that popular support for capital punishment for murder still extends to over two-thirds of the general population. However, weekly churchgoers endorse this view at a rather lower level (some 57% in 1994) (Gill, 1999, pp. 186–187).

Christian reflections on punishment

There are strong voices in the Christian tradition arguing either that the notion of retribution is sub-Christian or that it can only apply to God's judgement and not ours (cf. Romans 12:17–21). If Christians must always look to the possibility of good coming out of evil, it is hard to see how punishment can be justified except through its consequences.

Yet can we accept any theory of punishment that might justify the punishment of the innocent? The Bible insists that the innocent should not suffer (see Psalm 10; Amos 5:10–24; Micah 2 and 3). On a utilitarian view ends justify means; but this does not mean that *any* end can justify *every* means, and we may want to insist that some means cannot be justified at all, however good the results. Could any consequences justify treating human beings solely as a means to an end?

Perhaps no one account of punishment can provide an adequate justification by itself: 'The retributive theory, which is often taken to be an expression of barbarism, in fact provides a safeguard against the inhumane sacrifice of the individual for the social good, which is the moral danger in the utilitarian theory' (Downie, 1975, p. 227). Punishment must do some good; but it must also be *deserved*. Is this a proper Christian view?

Christian reflections on forgiveness

You may be wondering what has become of the great Christian theme of forgiveness in this discussion. In a sense there is no place for it. It is only the victim, and her family and friends, who can exercise forgiveness; the State is not in that position. And the victim can still forgive even as the State pursues its task of punishing the criminal. Forgiveness is in this sense 'personal'. It is also a character trait or virtue, relevant in debates about what sort of people we should be, but less relevant in an area where the ethical question is 'What ought we, as a society, to do?'

However, Christians should forgive. When Jesus speaks of our forgiving the 'debts' of others he takes us far beyond a legal context. 'The legal concept of a relationship of debt does not contain the idea of forgiveness or remission, and precludes any more comprehensive grounds than those which connect creditors with debtors' (Lohmeyer, 1965, p. 171). Jesus' teaching on forgiveness is radical: there should be no limit to our forgiveness of the injuries we suffer, for there is no limit to God's forgiveness of us (Matthew 6:12–15; 18:21–35; Mark 11:25). This is only possible, however, when and where human forgiveness is understood 'simply as a reflection of the divine forgiveness', as we 'hand on what we ourselves receive' (Lohmeyer, 1965, pp. 182, 187).

The dictionary defines forgiveness as a matter of stopping feeling angry or resentful towards someone for an offence or mistake. But in its religious heartland, forgiveness is more positive than that. It is understood there as a matter of 'covering' the offence or 'sending it away', and of actively restoring the sinner to fellowship. A state of forgiveness is a state of (restored) relationship. In human forgiveness too there is a need to 'do away with' the thing (the hurt or offence) that has come between the other person and ourselves.

The inadequacy of retribution is that the past disruption is not dealt with, not 'undone'. Christian theology will look for something more creative. Vernon White argues that this is 'so much more than the formal balance of suffering to mirror the balance of the past'; it means 'forging good out of all the interlocking consequences as they reach outward' (White, 1991, p. 105).

It is *possible* that punishment might fulfil this role, but perhaps only where the victim and the perpetrator of crime come into some sort of relationship. Dare we seek to promote *that*?

Further reading

Introductory
Adams, R (1998), *The Abuses of Punishment*, London, Macmillan.

Crawford, R (2000), *Can We Ever Kill?*, London, Darton, Longman and Todd, chapters 4 and 5.

Glover, J (1977, reprinted 1990), *Causing Death and Saving Lives*, Harmondsworth, Penguin, chapters 18 and 19.

Harries, R (1986), *Christianity and War in a Nuclear Age*, London, Mowbray.

Hospers, J (1972), *Human Conduct: problems of ethics*, New York, Harcourt Brace Jovanovich, chapter 20.

Vardy, P and Grosch, P (1994), *The Puzzle of Ethics*, London, HarperCollins, chapter 14.

Advanced
Bainton, R (1961), *Christian Attitudes towards War and Peace*, London, Hodder and Stoughton.

Bauchham, R and Elford, R J (eds) (1989), *The Nuclear Weapons Debate*, London, SCM.

Hauerwas, S (1984), *The Peaceable Kingdom: a primer in Christian ethics*, London, SCM.

Honderich, T (1984), *Punishment: the supposed justifications*, Harmondsworth, Penguin.

Moberly, W (1968), *The Ethics of Punishment*, London, Faber and Faber.

Teichman, J (1986), *Pacifism and the Just War*, Oxford, Blackwell.

8. DISAGREEING WITH OUR NEIGHBOURS

Introduction

Moral education may be said to begin with disagreement. As children we are told that some things that we do are 'bad' or 'naughty', and are often scolded or punished for them. If we had been born agreeing with our parents about the evaluation of all such actions, none of this would be necessary.

Of course, not all disagreement even about actions is *moral* disagreement. 'Stop it, you're hurting your sister' might be met with 'But she likes it.' This is a factual rather than a moral disagreement. The exchange: 'Don't tell lies', 'But it's true' would be another example. Sometimes, however, especially as we grow older, the disagreements are essentially about whether this act or principle is right, whether this situation or person is good. As we have in the end to decide for ourselves in such matters (for even letting others decide for us is our decision), we are often faced by the question, 'Do I agree with this moral claim, or not?'

Reflecting on experience

Imagine a conversation between two people who disagree over a moral issue such as euthanasia. What relevance does such disagreement have for our understanding of the nature of morality? In particular, what are you trying to do when you argue with someone about morality? And what does it mean if you come to 'agree to disagree'?

The overridingness of moral judgements

When you are suddenly faced by the *moral* dimension of a situation, everything changes. The discernment of a moral issue seems to override all other concerns. We feel that there is nothing more serious than a moral claim; nothing more significant than a disagreement over deeply held values. And yet people agree to disagree, at least sometimes.

One consideration is that morality can never just be a private thing. Moralities are shared and social. 'Front doors are indeed barriers . . . to unmannerly intrusion', writes Mary Midgley, 'but not to moral judgement. People who live in separate houses are still unavoidably members one of another' (Midgley, 1991, p. 62). Certain individualistic notions of moral independence or 'autonomy' reduce morality to the lone individual consulting her own conscience. The problem with that view is that 'such an interpretation turns morality into a wholly private affair', leaving no room for public morality and for 'what is morally right and morally wrong' (Baier, 1973, pp. 100–101). Naturally there are *some* judgements that are only morally relevant to a restricted circle of other people, such as some judgements about sexual behaviour, but the wholesale 'privatisation' of judgement turns morality into something else.

In *Can't We Make Moral Judgements?* Midgley faces a challenge that was once presented to her as a moral platitude: 'But surely it's always wrong to make moral judgements?' (Midgley, 1991, p. 1).

EXERCISE
How would you reply to this claim? What arguments can you pose both for and against it?

There are various reasons why people so often say this sort of thing.
- One factor is the spread of attitudes of tolerance and non-interference, and of respect for the autonomy of other people and their judgements.
- Another is their increasing suspicion of absolute moral claims, coupled with a recognition that morality is more relative, changing and human than was implied by the old authority figures and codes of behaviour.

• A third factor, I would suggest, is that our society is losing its nerve about moral education.

In this chapter we shall look at the first two of these factors, leaving discussion of moral education to Chapter 9.

The value and limits of tolerance

Tolerance is the willingness to endure ('tolerate') something. It is a virtue, for we should be humble in our judgements, acknowledging our ignorance about other people and their situations, and honouring their actions and character.

EXERCISE
Try to imagine two situations:
• one in which tolerance is clearly a virtue; and
• one in which it seems to be a vice or at least a mistake.

A classical problem situation is that of 'tolerance of intolerance'. When we find ourselves defending the freedom of speech or action of the racist, tolerance self-destructs. Tolerance is only a virtue if it is qualified and kept within certain limits. 'There is a time to tolerate and a time to fight' (Blackburn, 1998, p. 306). Some people only appeal to tolerance when they do not care much about the principles concerned (Almond, 1994, p. 165).

Note further that the notion of tolerance actually implies a degree of *disapproval* of the thing tolerated. Being tolerant is deciding not to act on that disapproval. Parents may tolerate their children's 'unsuitable friends', but the children themselves do not tolerate their friends – they approve of them! Necessarily, tolerance does not imply that all beliefs and practices are equally admirable. Only if you think some are worse than others is there anything to tolerate.

We are justifiably encouraged to be non-judgemental in many of our conversations and relationships. This maxim comes from counselling, a practice with its own (therapeutic) justification. But that is a particular context, created and protected for particular good ends. While the *counsellor* is right not to voice moral judgements about his clients, moral assessments can and should still be made about those situations that the client and counsellor are discussing.

Note that 'judging' other people morally, by evaluating their actions or their character, is not always the same thing as *blaming* them. After all, they may be ignorant or tempted beyond endurance. What do we know? When we engage in moral assessment, we are rarely condemning others as persons; nor are we claiming the last word, showing our moral superiority or being hypocritical (cf. Haydon, 1999, p. 92).

It *is* often morally admirable to be tolerant and not to intervene in other people's decisions and lives. But there are other attitudes, values and actions to which we should be committed that often conflict with the decision to tolerate a situation. Tolerance is not the sole, or the highest, virtue.

Responsibility and respect

At the end of John Braine's novel *Room at the Top*, Joe Lampton is overcome by guilt. He has finished his affair with the unhappily married Alice Aisgill, in favour of the younger, much wealthier and now pregnant Susan. Alice, after drinking all night, has run her car into a wall. Joe gets drunk himself and then into a fight. He is eventually picked up from the gutter by Bob and Eva Storr.

> I went on crying, as if the tears would blur the image of Alice crawling round Corby Road on her hands and knees, as if they would drown her first shrill screams and her last delirious moans. 'Oh, God', I said, 'I did kill her. I wasn't there, but I killed her.'
>
> Eva drew my head on to her breast. 'Poor darling, you mustn't take on so. You don't see it now, but it was all for the best. She'd have ruined your whole life. Nobody blames you, love. Nobody blames you.'
>
> I pulled myself away from her abruptly. 'Oh my God', I said, 'that's the trouble.' (Braine, 1989, p. 235)

EXERCISE

What interpretation would you place on Joe's words? Why is it no comfort to be told that no one blames him? Would you blame Joe?

Joe needs to feel responsible for what he has done, although Alice alone bears positive responsibility for her own actions. He feels that he deserves blame, that blame would make him more of a person rather than less of one. One of Kant's alternative formulations of his categorical imperative is relevant here also: that one should 'act in such a way that you always treat humanity, whether in your own person or in that of any other, never simply as a means but always at the same time as an end' (Kant, 1948, p. 91). Part of what that implies is that we should respect the dignity of others as free rational agents, capable of making their own decisions. But that involves holding them accountable for their decisions and actions, and treating their behaviour as subject to moral judgement.

Respect for others necessitates our taking them – with their different values – seriously, even though *respect for morality* necessitates our taking our own values seriously to the extent that we employ them as part of our moral standpoint from which we appraise, and sometimes criticise and reject, other people's values. Moral disagreement must be allowed, even between friends and within families. If we are to stay human, we must acknowledge what we believe to be right and wrong, good or bad.

Ethics as relative or subjective

Our contemporary 'erosion of values' is often blamed on philosophies that reject the view that morality is objective and absolute. *Moral realism* claims that morality reflects facts that are true independently of human decisions, beliefs or feelings; that moral values are 'out there' rather than 'in here' (in our hearts or minds). Morality may then be known by some form of moral vision, on the authority of revelation or by exercising our reason (*moral rationalism*). *Subjectivism* denies these claims about the objectivity of morals. *Relativism* denies the traditional absolutist view that moral truths are universal, rather than being relative to the people who voice them. (Moral principles may be regarded as 'absolute', however, in other senses: because they are seen as exceptionless or immutable.)

Types of relativism

The fact that Tibetans share wives between father and son, and we do not, is an expression of *cultural relativity*: the non-controversial claim that different societies think differently about ethics (and that our own society has during its history repeatedly changed its moral norms).

Moral relativism is much more controversial. It rejects the notion of absolute moral values, truths or principles of *universal application*. Moral relativists claim that morality is relative to the speaker's views, culture, social norms and so on. Your moral judgement is then true 'for you', but my different judgement, based on my different set of moral principles and attitudes, is true for me (or for *us* – for my society or culture). Relativism is often taken to imply that we cannot criticise the behaviour of other cultures, or indeed of our own, since whatever our society believes (presumably whatever the majority in it believes) is automatically right. Then 'good' simply means 'socially approved'.

EXERCISE
What arguments might be brought against this form of simple moral relativism?

Here are some common criticisms. *Empirically* ('factually') it just is not true that cultures do not share some basic moral values or principles. Rules like 'Do not kill the innocent' and 'Keep your promises' would seem to be necessary for any society. Many apparent moral differences are only differences about what counts as 'innocent' or 'a promise', masking agreement at the deeper level. Underlying this real moral unity is 'a common human nature': 'some basic structure indicating what kinds of things can be good and bad for human beings' (Midgley, 1991, pp. 85–86).

Logically ('philosophically') it does not follow from the fact of moral disagreement that there is no single moral truth. People used to disagree as to whether the earth was round but it was always true that it was. Further, the appeal to 'our society' is ambiguous. We are all members of a number of overlapping social groupings. Which one should I consult to decide whether racism is wrong?

Psychologically or phenomenologically (in terms of its nature as a phenomenon) morality seems to 'stand above' or transcend particular cultures, offering us independent moral standards that can be brought to bear to criticise or applaud *any* moral norms – including our own.

A naive moral relativism suggests that morality is just like etiquette. If torturing children for fun is only bad relative to our particular moral code, then morality does not really matter and we cannot judge other people's standards. *Postmodernism* professes that all truth is relative, indeed that there is no such thing as 'Truth' only 'truths', and that all claims to objectivity and rationality should be rejected as disguised assertions of power and privilege. This view can lead to scepticism about making any judgements and a readiness to accept any interpretation as being as good as any other. But note that, according to relativism, although it is not morally wrong for cannibals to be cannibals according to their moral framework ('it is not wrong *of them*'), cannibalism is wrong according to *our* moral framework. So we can still say, 'Cannibalism is wrong.'

More sophisticated, qualified forms of relativism accept that there are some moral criteria that are independent of different societies, so that moralities that result in more conflict within society or more selfish behaviour may be criticised. Further, according to some relativists, the moral framework in question here is not the actual rules of any individual or society, but their 'moral ideal' – what they would regard as an *adequate* set of moral rules.

David Wong points out that different types of morality are often based on different fundamental goods, for example individual rights and liberties in the West and community life and social rules in the East (Wong, 1993, pp. 445–446). Different cultures may quite rationally prize different goods for there is no rational route to resolving such disagreements.

Although relativism is the claim that moral truth is relative to our moral principles, Robert Arrington denies both that these are defined by social conventions and that there are 'alternative moralities'. On Arrington's view, basic moral principles are like rules of grammar: they determine what makes sense in (moral) language and thus *define* morality for us. They cannot be justified by reason but then they do not need to be. Morality is now not seen as relative to arbitrary social rules but to much more fundamental basic moral concepts. In this *conceptual relativism* we do not argue morally with young children or cannibals; we demand 'that they change their ways and become moral persons' by adopting the grammar of morality (Arrington, 1989, pp. 273–274).

Types of subjectivism

Subjectivism is the view that our morality is based on something about us, rather than some objective truth. At its simplest, the theory suggests that moral judgements are just statements about our attitudes or feelings: 'This is wrong' then means 'I disapprove of this.'

EXERCISE

How adequate is this account of morality? How may the theory be improved, while keeping the focus on feelings?

One problem is that this account cannot explain moral disagreement. 'I disapprove of this war', said by Graham, does not contradict Sarah's statement that she approves of it. Values are here no more than personal preferences.

Emotivism claims that moral assertions are not statements at all but expressions of our feelings or attitudes. Expressions, unlike statements, can be neither true nor false. 'Abortion is wrong' is then understood not as a statement about a moral truth or about the speaker's state of mind, but as an expression of distaste and disapproval of abortion, equivalent to 'Abortion? Yuk!' or 'Boo for abortion' or (probably) something much stronger. Now, people can disagree *in* their attitudes: in this case some are in favour of a situation where abortion happens, others want one where there is no abortion (cf. Price, 1969, pp. 400–412).

If subjectivism can allow for disagreement, can it also allow for the exercise of reason? The *ideal spectator theory* argues that for me to say that an act is right is to say, not that *I* approve of it, but that an ideal (impartial and fully informed, sympathetic, fully rational and consistent) observer would approve of it. That gives me a good reason for approving of it. A moral claim is now no longer an expression of my attitudes and feelings, however, but a statement about the best set of attitudes to adopt and the decent (the right) thing to feel.

Sophisticated subjectivist views (sometimes called *expressivism*) recognise that values are not just preferences and that to acknowledge that something is good is not simply to like it. Condemning racism is not at the same level as a distaste for peanut butter! Unlike taste preferences, moral judgements are *prescriptive* (they prescribe what other people ought to do and to feel) and *universalisable*. The attitudes evoked in moral situations are 'more strident' ones, which make us 'wish disfavoured actions discouraged by some kind of social sanction' (Sprigge, 1988, p. 61).

Simon Blackburn agrees that you can always ask of any feeling or desire whether it is morally 'good' or not, just as you can ask of any perception whether it is an illusion or not, but he argues that you can only do so by relying on other feelings as you can only judge illusions by relying on other perceptions. He contends that 'we judge oughts ... because of the shape of our prescriptions and attitudes and stances, because of our desires, and because of our emotional natures.' But this is 'something that is true' (Blackburn, 1998, p. 320). He allows for talk of 'moral truths', although they are not like truths in physics, and of 'moral knowledge' ('to indicate that a judgement is beyond revision', p. 318). For such a sophisticated exponent, morality is not *simply* non-factual ('non-cognitive') and subjective.

Universal morality

Morality demands a universal rule. We feel that there should only be one 'right' morality, despite the apparent variety of moral positions.

EXERCISE
Some claim that a common set of core values is to be found in the teachings of the different religions. Do you agree? What might they be?

The Chicago 1993 meeting of the Parliament of the World's Religions agreed a declaration on *The Principles of a Global Ethic*, which it described as 'a minimum fundamental consensus concerning binding values, irrevocable standards, and fundamental moral attitudes'. The basic demand that it endorsed was that 'every human being must be treated humanely.' This was said to find expression in a principle common to many religious and ethical traditions, the golden rule of 'what you wish done to yourself, do to others'. This 'irrevocable, unconditional norm' for all was defined in concrete terms by reference to *four comprehensive, ancient imperatives of humanity*, said to be found in most religions (Küng and Schmidt, 1998, pp. 7–33):

- the commitment to non-violence and reverence for life (traditionally expressed in the command 'You shall not kill');
- the commitment to solidarity and a just economic order ('You shall not steal');
- the commitment to tolerance and living with truth ('You shall not lie');
- the commitment to equality and partnership between men and women, and to love and respect for one another ('You shall not commit sexual immorality').

Human rights

The quest for a universal morality is often connected with the language of human rights, as expressed in the writings of John Locke, the American 'Declaration of Independence', the French National Assembly's 'Declaration of the Rights of Man and of the Citizen', and Thomas Paine's *The Rights of Man* (1791).

Rights may be defined as powers or privileges to which an individual has a just claim and can demand that they be not suspended or infringed; they are 'the strongest kind of claim there is' (Wasserstrom, 1975a, p. 111). (The language of 'having rights' is not to be confused with the moral judgement that an action is 'right'. We may have a right to do something which could be morally wrong in a particular situation, and we often have no right to do something which would be the 'right thing to do'.)

Some writers distinguish 'inalienable' and 'exceptionless' (or 'absolute') rights from other rights that are lower in rank and may be overruled, especially in extreme situations and when two rights are in conflict. Rights are often appealed to in moral discussion:
• as prior to States and their laws (which may be unjust);
• as a feature of our common humanity, independent of 'contingent' factors such as our colour, sex or social status;
• as able to compel compliance, enforcement or at least certain safeguards.

Some rights correlate with obligations, so that if you have a right to something there is an obligation for someone to supply it; but many duties – for example benevolence – do not confer rights on the recipient.

EXERCISE

Make a list of things that you would regard as *universal* 'human rights'.

Do you think that the idea of human rights fits or conflicts with Christian morality?

Philosophers sometimes distinguish between two types of rights:
• rights of action ('liberties', 'privileges' or 'powers') or active rights, which are our rights to do things; and

- rights of recipience ('claims' or 'immunities') or passive rights, which are our rights to have things done to or for us; these are rights that others should provide or do something about.

Every active right implies a passive right that others should not interfere with the exercise of this right. R S Downie argues that all human rights are rights of recipience, for we have no right to do what we like with our liberty but our liberty should not be interfered with in certain ways. He limits human rights to *universal, practicable and paramount* rights, cutting out (for example) the right to holidays with pay because that right would be dependent on the existence of a wage-earning economy. He then argues that all such rights reduce to *liberty* and *equality*. Respect for persons as ends in themselves gives each person a right to self-realisation (and therefore liberty) and a right to equal treatment (and therefore equality, in the context of distributive justice) (Downie, 1971, pp. 51–53).

While some still regard rights as self-evident to reason, or derived from divine law or a social contract, others have declared them 'fictions' or even 'nonsense upon stilts' (Bentham). Mary Warnock objects to the whole notion as bestowing a quasi-legal force and air of certainty on what are, in fact, disputable moral principles. 'Why should we not prefer simply to talk about ways in which it would be right or wrong, good or bad, to treat our fellow humans?' (Warnock, 1998, p. 63).

Christian criticisms

Many Christians value the philosophy of human rights as vesting the worth of individuals 'in their common humanity rather than their differences' (White, 1996, p. 37). But it has also been criticised on a number of grounds.

- It is a limited notion, unlikely to generate unselfishness, altruism, pity or sacrifice: 'the demands of love . . . exceed the demands of fairness' (Baelz, 1977, p. 72).
- Christian ethics, it has been said, should generate a shift from our rights to our duties, 'from claiming to giving one's own' (Ramsey, 1953, p. 354). Other people are our neighbours; we should be more concerned to meet their claims than to assert our own rights over against them as if they were adversaries.
- The appropriate response to infringed rights is indignation. This is in conflict with the Christian call to forgive.
- Rhetoric about human rights can be too assertive and demanding, and often ignores our duty of exercising our rights responsibly.

- It expresses an essentially individualistic idea. What about the rights of society?

Many of these objections can be met if we focus on the rights of *others* rather than on our own rights. In that case, a claim to rights is a claim that others possess rights 'in me', as duties that I owe to my neighbour 'for Christ's sake' (Ramsey, 1953, p. 187).

What do you think?

Further reading

Introductory

Gensler, H J (1998), *Ethics: a contemporary introduction*, London, Routledge, chapters 1, 2 and 5.

Küng, H (1991), *Global Responsibility: in search of a new world ethic*, ET London, SCM.

Midgley, M (1991), *Can't We Make Moral Judgements?*, Bristol, Bristol Press.

Robinson, D and Garratt, R (1999), *Introducing Ethics*, Cambridge, Icon.

Vardy, P and Grosch, P (1994), *The Puzzle of Ethics*, London, HarperCollins, chapter 15.

Warnock, M (1998), *An Intelligent Person's Guide to Ethics*, London, Duckworth, chapter 6.

Advanced

Cronin, K (1992), *Rights and Christian Ethics*, Cambridge, Cambridge University Press.

Downie, R S (1971), *Roles and Values: an introduction to social ethics*, London, Methuen.

Harman, G (1977), *The Nature of Morality: an introduction to ethics*, New York, Oxford University Press.

Hebblethwaite, B (1997), *Ethics and Religion in a Pluralistic Age*, Edinburgh, T and T Clark.

MacNaughton, D (1988), *Moral Vision: an introduction to ethics*, Oxford, Blackwell.

Williams, B (1972), *Morality: an introduction*, Cambridge, Cambridge University Press.

9. TEACHING RIGHT FROM WRONG

Introduction

Whenever you read this book, you will be able to reflect on some current controversy about moral education. Someone, somewhere – usually a politician – will be complaining that the home or the school, the two most important places where we learn to be moral, are failing in their task. 'Something must be done', he or she will demand, 'our children need to be taught the difference between right and wrong.'

Well, we have all been children. What has been our experience?

> *Reflecting on experience*
> What factors most influenced your moral development? How important were your parents, peers, teachers and others?

Moral development

That word 'development' may be understood as referring to two rather different sorts of change in your moral beliefs, values, insights or understanding. The first represents changes brought about by an *experience from which you learned*. But a second type of change is brought about by some *internal process of growth or maturation*. In this section we shall concentrate on the second category: change that originates within a person.

A number of psychologists have attempted to trace a developmental pattern undergirding morality so as to explain some of the transformations in a child's moral reasoning as she matures. Within the cognitive developmental tradition in psychology two figures dominate the scene: Jean Piaget and Lawrence Kohlberg.

Piaget explored the nature of children's moral judgements by talking with children between the ages of four and twelve about their attitudes to rules and their notions of justice and fairness, as well as their own judgements of right and wrong. He found that young children regarded behaviour as right if adults approved of it and judged actions by their consequences rather than the agent's intention. Around the age of eleven, however, they gradually moved from this heteronomous, 'conventional' stage of morality to a less rigid 'rational morality', in which they formulated their own moral rules by mutual agreement and applied them according to circumstances. This change results, Piaget claimed, from a process of cognitive restructuring of the way they think morally (Piaget, 1932).

Building on the suggestions of Piaget and his own extensive research, Kohlberg argued that as the child matures the structures of her moral thinking and understanding move through a series of six possible stages of irreversible development, in interaction with her environment (Kohlberg, 1981): from interpreting morality as a matter of doing what you are told, through stages of conventional moral reasoning, to a morality of self-accepted moral principles. Progression through the stages may be aided through the 'cognitive stimulation' provided by facing the child with new challenges, experiences or complex stimuli that her present stage of development cannot fully grasp.

Education in values

Education takes us beyond such psychological development to a consideration of learning-changes brought about by experience. Moral education envisages a number of different types of changes. Four common approaches may be distinguished (Halstead and Taylor, 1996, chapter 1).

- **'Character education'** consists of the moral formation of children by means of the transmission of values.
- **'Values education'** – often called 'values clarification' – involves the pupil in exploring and developing his or her own values.
- **The 'moral reasoning'** approach helps students to develop higher levels of moral reasoning through discussing dilemmas.
- **The 'just community'** approach strives to develop responsible behaviour by children sharing group norms in community.

Values education: for and against

This is the most controversial approach. In values education children are assisted 'to make explicit those values underlying their own behaviour, to assess the effectiveness of these values and associated behaviour for their own and others' long term well-being and to reflect on and acquire other values and behaviour' which they recognise as being more effective for that well-being (Robb, 1994, p. 5). The process enables children to make up their own minds about morality: 'people are not told how to think or behave' and 'the teacher's views carry no more authority than the young people's' (Robb, 1996, p. 24). Its supporters describe this as the best way of developing responsible behaviour.

EXERCISE

What are the likely strengths and weaknesses of values education?

The 'procedural neutrality' of this approach, in which the teacher exercises the role of a 'neutral chairman' in moral debate, has been criticised by many. Such criticism may sometimes be unfair, for teacher neutrality is usually proposed only for significantly controversial matters (McLaughlin, 1995, p. 23). Yet, as Mary Warnock writes, 'teaching is an essentially moral transaction', at least insofar as it demands the transmission of 'classroom virtues' and of the common 'civil or societal values' which form the basis of society (Warnock, 1996, pp. 49, 52, 53). Elsewhere she writes:

> The teacher must know what is right and what is wrong, must confidently draw the distinction for her pupils, and in the matter of their behaviour, must give praise or blame to what deserves it. (Warnock, 1998, p. 121)

David Carr believes that there is value in both the 'traditional-paternalist' and the 'liberal-progressive' conceptions of moral education, approaches that are broadly equivalent to our 'character education' and 'values education'. But he sees more of a danger in the liberal style of moral education.

> The deep truth expressed by liberalism is that morality is a sphere in which freedom of thought and conduct is of undeniable significance; any moral education worthy of the name must therefore be one in

which young people are equipped with capacities for wise and principled decisions about how they will live their lives, as well as with some
sense of personal responsibility for their own decisions. But in the
course of affirming the moral primacy of freedom and resisting
that which might threaten to inhibit it, liberal views often seem to
have gone overboard in endorsing a certain agnosticism about moral
truth. . . . [and the] view that if the choices of young people are to be
really free, then we should refrain from their instruction in any moral
attitudes and conduct on pain of jeopardising that freedom. (Carr,
1996b, p. 10)

As we saw in the last chapter, our account of the nature of morality
and of moral education needs to stay close to the distinctive phenomenology and grammar of morality. It must therefore honour the sense:
• that morality is somehow a matter of truth;
• that it gives rise to criticism and supports argument;
• that it is *not just* an expression of what the moral speaker thinks or
feels; and
• that it is in principle universalisable.

It is not surprising, therefore, that even the sophisticated relativist
and the sophisticated expressivist acknowledge that ethics has a certain
sort of 'objectivity', 'cognitivity' or even 'absoluteness' (see above
pp. 92–94). They can therefore agree with more traditional accounts of
morality over the importance of *transmitting* morality and forming
children in the moral life. We might argue that if we do not wish to
share our moral values with our children, then very probably they are
not really 'values' to us at all.

EXERCISE

Imagine (or remember!) that you are bringing up a young child.
Would you feel justified in 'passing on' your morality to her?
• If not, why not, and where will she get her values from?
• If so, what is there to 'pass on' and how might this best be done?

Multi-dimensional moral formation

I would argue that a large part of moral education in schools, families,
Churches and other social institutions and groups is made up of what
we might call *moral formation*: processes that lead to the learning of

moral values, principles, dispositions and so on. This formation is often implicit and unacknowledged as a learning process, as when a young child 'models' her behaviour on that of her parents or other significant figures (including fictional characters). At other times moral formation will be a much more self-consciously educational experience of learning and reflection. This reflection will lead naturally into *critical moral education*, in which moral principles and arguments are debated and evaluated (see the next section).

Morality is itself *multi-dimensional*. Thus even a simple moral 'speech-act', such as 'that is wrong', does a number of different things (cf. Brümmer, 1981, p. 117).

- It *expresses* the attitude we have to that act or situation and by implication would have to all such acts or situations.
- It *prescribes* the attitude others should have to that act or situation.
- It *commits* us to a norm of being for (or against) all such acts or situations.
- It *implies* that that act or situation is an example of this norm and (most would claim) that certain other facts are true – for example facts about the existence of a value or the will of God.

Formative moral education covers an even wider range of dimensions. Moral formation will induct children into (help them to learn) nine elements: norms, virtues, attitudes and feelings, reasoning, vision, actions, community, exemplars and (for Christians) theology.

Norms or rules of conduct
These are prescriptive standards or imperatives (for example 'Don't lie' and 'Don't harm the innocent') and fundamental moral concepts or principles (more general considerations such as 'fairness' or 'respect'). Some of these things may be said to define morality: 'in instructing [children] that one ought not to tell a lie and that one ought to keep promises, one is introducing them to morality' (Arrington, 1989, pp. 273–274). For many, this is the most important component of moral education.

Character dispositions or virtues
Virtue ethics would place more emphasis on teaching morally desirable personal qualities than on teaching moral rules. Its advocates argue that the highest task of education is 'the job of acquainting [children] with those homely and familiar human excellences called the moral virtues – honesty, tolerance, fairmindedness, courage, persistence, consideration,

patience and so forth'. The schools that do this best are those with virtuous teachers, where 'children are taught by teachers who are themselves clearly committed to integrity, truth and justice and who have sought to transform the school and the classroom into the kinds of communities where a love of what is right, decent and good is exhibited as often as possible in the conduct of those into whose care they have been given' (Carr, 1991, p. 269).

EXERCISE
Think of those schoolteachers who most influenced you. What was it about them that you remember? In what sense were they 'models' of being human and being moral?

Other attitudes and feelings

The last category clearly overlaps with a whole range of other elements, such as 'friendliness', 'trust' and 'outrage', that make up the moral disposition. Following Aristotle, Roger Scruton argues that knowing what to do also involves feeling rightly. 'The virtuous person "knows what to feel", and this means feeling what the situation requires: the right emotion, towards the right object, on the right occasion and in the right degree. Moral education has just such knowledge as its goal: it is an education of the emotions' (Scruton, 1998, p. 15). Simon Blackburn is even more insistent that moral education is a 'sentimental education':

> We educate people to care that they share the desires we admire . . . We can exhort the knave to share our sentiments. We can try to turn up the volume of his feelings for those whom he exploits . . . The subject is brought to feel that dishonesty, or exploitation, or discounting outsiders, will not do. (Blackburn, 1998, p. 209)

If morality evaluates both *the act* and *the agent*, both types of valuation need to find expression in a full moral education that addresses both an ethic of norms and an ethic of virtue or character. Some educationalists would argue, however, that norms lend themselves better to a public articulation of shared values, and therefore to moral education, than do the rather more personal and contentious virtues (cf. Haydon, 1999, pp. 61, 150).

> **EXERCISE**
> Do you agree with this claim? Is the classroom more conducive to developing an ethic of obligation ('Do this . . .') than to developing an ethic of virtues ('Be this . . .')?
>
> Is the home different?

Ways of moral thinking

There must be room for reasoning in ethics, if only about the effects of different actions. Haydon offers a broader set of guidelines for moral reasoning that pupils should be encouraged to consider whenever they make a moral decision (Haydon, 1999, p. 79).

1. Be aware of the ways in which what you are doing is going to affect other people. Think about this if it is not obvious.
2. Try to think yourself into the position of other people affected by what you are doing: try to see what it is like to be in their shoes.
3. Think whether they would be likely to agree to what you are doing. Sometimes, the appropriate way of doing this will be to ask them. If that is not possible, you can still ask yourself 'if I were in their position, would I agree to be on the receiving end of the kind of thing which I, now, am thinking of doing?' (E.g. if you have in mind to do something which involves deceiving another person, ask yourself whether you could agree to be deceived in a situation like this.)
4. Having seen what it would be like to be in the position of each of the people affected – seeing it, if you can, as if it were happening to you – ask yourself whether you think it is all right for people, in the sort of situation you are in now, to do the kind of thing you are thinking of doing.

We may also consider moral reasoning at a more fundamental level. If someone believes, for example, that the eye colour of the mother is relevant to a discussion of the morality of abortion, he simply does not understand how to think morally (see Chapter 1). An induction into the logic and skills of moral reasoning probably happens very early in education, in the home rather than the school. Without it, the child would be as puzzled about moral discussion as the businessman played by

John Cleese in the famous sketch, who remained totally confused by the financial transaction that the charity collector was suggesting ('Yes, I see what the *orphans* get out of this, but . . .').

'Moral vision'

This outcome of moral education may be understood in a variety of ways: as a perception of objective moral value, as seeing 'a different world' (Murdoch, 1992, p. 177), or simply as a particular 'onlook' or affective 'take' on people or events (for example seeing others *as* children of God). In this area, moral education is analogous to some aspects of education in literature or the arts, where the teacher tries to get the learners to 'see things differently'.

Dispositions to engage in moral actions

Morality is essentially an activity, so developing a disposition to act morally must be another essential outcome of moral learning, not least because our actions have a role in learning as we act ourselves into different ways of feeling and valuing. Hence von Hügel's claim that 'I kiss my child not only because I love her, but in order to love her' and Aristotle's argument that we learn the virtues by practising them.

Membership of a community

Many would stress the importance in moral education of feeling you belong to a community of shared judgements, reasoning, values, attitudes and feelings. This helps learners to see themselves as 'on the inside of morality'. Graham Haydon develops the point:

> One of the most important tasks for education where morality is concerned is to try to overcome the alienation that many people may feel from their community . . . A person can care about norms and care about adhering to them, if they are the norms of a community which he or she is part of and values. And then both the consciousness of the fact that these are shared values (where the fact that a society has shared values may itself be valued), and the consciousness of having played some part in the forming of a shared sense of values, can be positive factors in motivating persons to take such values more seriously, in the sense of seeing them as having authority over their own conduct. (Haydon, 1999, pp. 119–121)

Moral examples

Virtue ethics would also stress the importance of developing an acquaintance with individuals and communities that exemplify the virtues, and with the community's stories of moral exemplars and heroes, for 'learning to be as they are' (Hauerwas, 1980, p. 445).

EXERCISE

Traditional cultures passed on many stories of heroic acts and exemplary figures. It is often said that modern cultures are too cynical and critical to allow much of this. In your view, what figures do children and young people morally admire from history, fiction and the contemporary world? What values do these figures exemplify?

Knowledge of the will and character of God

Christian education in home and Church should include some appeal to Scripture and Christian tradition in the child's formative environment, as well as providing Christian versions of all the other dimensions of moral education.

Critical moral education

Is all this moral formation just too much, however? Do you now picture the child as rather swamped by the transmission of all these dimensions of morality; and wonder how she will ever learn to think morally for herself?

Those who insist that education should recognise 'the autonomy of the learner' often dismiss formative moral education in favour of encouraging moral criticism. In fact, both are needed. Children can only reach autonomy after a process of formation; and the learner is only truly formed in and converted to values when they become *her* values. Bear in mind that moral criticism can only be launched from a platform of moral principles and insights, so critical moral education can only take place within a framework of moral formation or nurture. This situation is quite normal and natural to social beings, and should not be rejected as 'indoctrination' or 'interference' (Carr, 1991, p. 243; Midgley, 1991, p. 58). Some have therefore defended a non-critical phase or element of formation and nurture in a child's moral education along the road to moral autonomy (Astley, 1994, chapter 5; Thiessen, 1993).

Moral education involves an interpretative conversation – in the jargon, a 'hermeneutical dialogue' – between the learner's experience and the moral tradition. As the learner, I am always in the centre of the frame and (particularly as I grow older) I will *inevitably* reflect critically on and judge the values I receive, including those that I eventually embrace. Formal education should certainly help to support this process.

EXERCISE

How far, and at what stage, should children be encouraged to be critical of the moral tradition in which they are formed?

Are there any dangers in adopting a critical stance towards morality?

In my view, there must be some limits to the openness and criticism that we encourage in our children's moral education. The reason for this is that some moral principles are necessarily highly resistant to criticism. We certainly do not want our children to be so tentative in their moral values that they are willing to change them on the basis of every so-called 'argument' and any piece of apparent 'evidence'. But is it enough to encourage children to be rationally moral: sharp in assessing arguments and weighing data? A parent who educates her children to be racially unprejudiced is implicitly teaching them that *nothing* should *ever* count as a 'good reason' against this view. This is not irrational for no argument or evidence is relevant to a deep moral principle like this. After all, what *could* possibly justify the adoption of a racist attitude to others?

In some areas (though not all) we want people to be as firm in their moral beliefs as they are about the reliability of Nature – or the goodness of God (Astley, 1994, p. 67).

What do you think?

Further reading

Introductory

Bottery, M (1990), *The Morality of the School: the theory and practice of values in education*, London, Cassell.

Clouse, B (1985), *Moral Development: perspectives in psychology and Christian belief*, Grand Rapids, Michigan, Baker Book House.

Coles, R (1997), *The Moral Intelligence of Children*, London, Bloomsbury.

Dykstra, C R (1981), *Vision and Character: a Christian educator's alternative to Kohlberg*, New York, Paulist.

Advanced

Astley, J (1994), *The Philosophy of Christian Religious Education*, Birmingham, Alabama, Religious Education Press, chapters 4, 5 and 9.

Halstead, M and Taylor, M J (eds) (1996), *Values in Education and Education in Values*, London, Falmer.

Haydon, G (1997), *Teaching about Values: a new approach*, London, Cassell.

Munsey, B (ed.), (1980), *Moral Development, Moral Education, and Kohlberg*, Birmingham, Alabama, Religious Education Press.

Smith, R and Standish, P (eds) (1997), *Teaching Right and Wrong: moral education in the balance*, Stoke on Trent, Trentham.

Van der Ven, J A (1998), *Formation of the Moral Self*, Grand Rapids, Michigan, Eerdmans.

Wilson, J (1990), *A New Introduction to Moral Education*, London, Cassell.

10. RELIGION AND MORAL CHOICE

Introduction

This book has explored ethical thinking and moral dilemmas both as areas of discussion in their own right and with reference to the Christian Gospel. But how should we think of the relationship between morality and Christianity, and how far may we treat our moral values as Christian values?

Reflecting on experience
What do *you* really value? Make a note of the five or six aspects of human life, and qualities of human action and character, that you value most highly.

The relationship between ethics and religion

'You don't have to be a Christian to be good.' But 'You do have to be good to be a Christian.' Religion, apparently, incorporates ethics and yet most would claim that ethics is separable from religion. Surely, ethics stands alone, it is autonomous. It is not just religious people who are, and ought to be, good. But does the unbeliever *sin*? Sin is essentially a religious category, marking an act of rebellious disobedience towards God. (In the Old Testament it is applied to ritual uncleanness that is an affront to God, as well as to 'moral sins' that additionally harm other people.) The concept of sin cannot replace the concept of immorality.

In tracing the relationship between religion and morality, a number of different positions have been defended. One view is that morality is to be identified with religion: either because religion is really just morality or because an act is right only because God commands it. Alternatively, morality and religion may be regarded as two separate things that are connected in some way or another.

Reducing religion to morality

Many people still mean by 'being Christian' simply 'doing good': for them Christianity is in reality nothing but morality (cf. Hoggart, 1957, pp. 116–119). Robert Towler labels this *exemplarism*: a 'moral type of religiousness', often unchurched and private, doctrinally agnostic or even atheistic, which sees in Jesus an example for all to follow (Towler, 1984, chapter 2). A much more sophisticated version of this reductionism was developed by Richard Braithwaite (1955) and Richard Hare (1992, chapters 1 and 2). It has been detected – perhaps unfairly – in some aspects of the work of Don Cupitt (Cupitt, 1988).

Morality dependent on religion: revisiting divine commands

'If there is a God, his being determines what is morally right or wrong' for 'the order of values is identical with the being of God' (Ward, 1976, p. 112; 1970, p. 107). The divine command theory (see Chapter 3) is a 'voluntarist' account of obligation, identifying the moral good with God's *will* and what is right with what God commands. An act is wrong, on this view, if it is forbidden by God and *because* it is forbidden by God. Some exponents add that the atheist can still know what is right without knowing God's commands; others deny this.

In Plato's dialogue the *Euthyphro* (10a) the following question is posed: 'Do the gods love holiness because it is holy, or is it holy because they love it?'

EXERCISE

How would you respond to the Euthyphro dilemma? Would you do it:

1. by claiming that God commands us to do only what is right; or
2. by claiming that whatever God commands is right?

What are the strengths and weaknesses of each of these replies?

If you adopt reply (1), as Kant did (1948, p. 73), you will seem to accept that the good is somehow 'prior' to God and has to be recognised by God. This would mean that we evaluate God against some independent moral scale.

Reply (2), which was the view taken by William of Ockham, presents other difficulties. It implies that things are neither good nor bad until God wills them: God's willing or commanding something *makes* it good. It would seem that anything could in principle be good on this view; morality depends on what God arbitrarily wills. If God instructs us to torture children tomorrow, that would become our duty. Some have said that whoever is ordering this it could not be God, for that would be inconsistent with God's nature as perfectly loving. But is this answer satisfactory? You may feel that there is something circular about it, since 'loving' is implicitly defined in terms of 'doing good' to someone and what is good is dependent on what God commands.

A more popular solution begins with reply (1) but adds that there is only one kind of life that is ultimately fulfilling for humans and that is what God requires of us. Even the atheist John Mackie applauded a solution in which 'the picture of God as an arbitrary tyrant is replaced by the belief that he demands of his creatures only that they should live in what will be, for them, the most satisfying way' (Mackie, 1977, p. 231). But our life is best satisfied by a relationship with God, who is 'the only proper and real end of all human striving' (Vardy, 1992, p. 106). So God is held to be good as the supremely worthwhile human goal.

What we value depends on the sort of nature we have and what will fulfil it. But the doctrine of creation claims that it is *God* who has given us this nature (through evolution). So when we judge God, God is describing himself as good 'through us'.

On this account, morality has its ultimate origin in God, yet our moral insights are really ours and may be held independently of any belief in or knowledge of God. (In the same way, although the chemical properties of our cells are ultimately determined by God, biochemists can study them without any reference to God at all.) Thus morality may be properly described as human and autonomous, although at a deeper level it is dependent on God's (hidden) creative act.

Separating morality and religion: revisiting natural law

There are those who argue, with Bishop Holloway, that we must disconnect religion from the struggle to create a 'genuinely ecumenical ethic' that can appeal to religious people and atheists alike. He claims that 'the attempt by humans to discuss a morality apart from God might, paradoxically, be God's greatest triumph' (Holloway, 1999, p. 5).

Natural law theory (see Chapter 3) tells us to use our (God-given) reason to discover the (God-given) natural purposes of things. For the unbeliever, however, the phrase 'God-given' will stay in brackets; she will just exercise her reason. Conscience, Aquinas says, is simply 'a certain dictate of reason' (*Summa Theologiae*, 1ae2ae, 19, 5; Vol. 18, 1966, p. 61). Natural law theory seems to make morality *in practice* independent of religion: a realm of autonomous truths that may be discerned by reason quite apart from belief in God. And the same can be said of my preferred solution to the *Euthyphro* dilemma on p. 111 above.

EXERCISE
How do you respond to these different ways of accommodating the moral atheist?

Connecting morality and religion

While it is unquestionably true that ethical reflection antedates Christianity, and that it increasingly takes place outside a religious context and without using theological vocabulary, most theologians would maintain that *Christian ethics* cannot be separated from Christian doctrine. 'Moral theology' is a proper part of theology and the moral life for the Christian is part of the spiritual life, involving the Christian's conformity to God and the renewal of her mind, heart and will in God. In the New Testament at least, talk about God, especially about our love towards and service of God, is inextricably linked with our love towards and service of one another. Christians contend that faith in Christ makes a moral difference and that the *sanctification* of the Christian, the work of God as Spirit co-operating with the human soul as the Christian 'lives into her baptism', is in part a process of moral growth.

EXERCISE
In what ways might Christian doctrine, particularly its beliefs about God, relate to the moral life?

Morality may be seen as logically implied by theology, provided that values can be derived from facts. The ethical implications of religious belief are relatively uncontroversial in the case of beliefs about what God commands. However, the claim is usually extended to other beliefs about the nature and activity of God, and the nature and destiny of human existence. The connection can then be more problematic. Beliefs about how we ought to behave may seem to follow reasonably readily from some beliefs about God's moral character (loving) and activity (creating, saving) (Gustafson, 1981, pp. 235–251). Theologians also claim that the trinitarian nature of God, as a community of love, has clear ethical implications (Grenz, 1997, pp. 261–262, 283–285, 293–297). But the connection is less obvious for other doctrines, such as God's transcendence or eternity.

On one view, Christian ethics is simply an account of the way of life that is appropriate for one who believes in a dependable Christ-like God. It is 'the way in which anyone who genuinely and wholeheartedly believes in the heavenly Father will naturally tend to live' (Hick, 1983, p. 63). This would be true of our more spiritual attitudes also, such as a trustful lack of anxiety about the future (cf. Matthew 6:25–34). The most general moral response to the question, 'What is God enabling and requiring us to be and to do', answered from a 'theocentric' (God-centred) understanding, is that 'we are to relate ourselves and all things in a manner appropriate to their relations to God' (Gustafson, 1981, p. 327).

Revisiting life and death

In considering ethical problems associated with life and death, orthodox Christians are likely to make reference to their belief that death is not the end of a person's existence and that injustices may be compensated by God after death. Such reflections will lead some to argue both that it is the 'quality' (or just the 'intrinsic value') of a human life that is significant, rather than any measure of its 'quantity', and that there *are* worse fates than death. 'Do not fear those who kill the body but cannot kill the soul; rather fear him who can destroy both soul and body in hell' (Matthew 10:28). However it is interpreted, this text suggests that a religious believer may have a different moral view of certain human actions.

Revisiting the ethics of response

In *The Freedom of a Christian*, Martin Luther wrote that the Christian ought to argue:

Although I am an unworthy and condemned man, my God has given me in Christ all the riches of righteousness and salvation without any merit on my part, out of pure, free mercy, so that from now on I need nothing except faith which believes that this is true. Why should I not therefore freely, joyfully, with all my heart, and with an eager will do all things which I know are pleasing and acceptable to such a Father who has overwhelmed me with his inestimable riches? I will therefore give myself as a Christ to my neighbor, just as Christ offered himself to me; I will do nothing in this life except what I see is necessary, profitable, and salutary to my neighbor, since through faith I have an abundance of all good things in Christ. (Dillenberger, 1961, p. 75)

EXERCISE

What do you think of Luther's view of the relationship between morality and theology?

Theology may be seen as the motivation for morality. Christian ethics is often regarded as a response of gratitude, and appreciation of God's acts is said to stimulate and empower a righteousness that exceeds reciprocity (see Chapter 3). In the Old Testament, Israel's election through God's grace is to be answered by her grateful obedience to God's demands: 'God has done this for you, therefore you should . . .' (cf. Leviticus 19:2; 19:34). Similarly, the New Testament's 'ethic of the Kingdom' is not a legalistic obedience to laws but rather an ethic of response to the grace-ful God and his redemptive work in Christ (cf. Matthew 5:44–45; Colossians 3:1, 13; 2 Corinthians 8:8–9). In the biblical logic of gratitude the *imperative* follows the *indicative*. 'God is . . .' and 'God did . . .' leads to 'you should be/do . . .', with 'therefore' as the key connecting word.

EXERCISE

📖 **Skim read Paul's letter to the Romans,** preferably in a version with sub-headings or topics printed at the top of each page. Can you find this structure in it?

- 1:18 to 3:20: human sin;
- 3:21 to 8:39: but the grace of God; ▶▶

> • 12:1 to 15:13: therefore the Christian ethic.
> (Chapters 9 to 11 represent an excursus on the theology of the Jews' rejection of Christ.)

Revisiting values: morality and spirituality

Religious people often argue that we can identify *spiritual values* that are distinct from ('merely') moral values. 'Holiness' has been suggested as an obvious example. According to one definition, spirituality comprises those attitudes, values, beliefs and practices that 'animate people's lives and help them to reach out towards super-sensible realities' (Wakefield, 1983, p. 549). On another, it is a matter of letting go of 'narcissism' (self-obsession) and surrendering oneself into the 'Mystery out of which everything arises' (Evans, 1993, pp. 1, 4). Such a spiritual standpoint is not just an expression of moral character, yet it is in principle not restricted to those who believe in God.

David Carr argues that spiritual virtues go beyond their moral counterparts, as 'hope' is more than 'courage' and 'asceticism' more than 'temperance'. They do this, he claims, in a way that relates to their being 'orientated . . . to what lies beyond the purely temporal' (Carr, 1995, p. 92). While others are happy to speak of non-religious (for example humanist and Marxist) spiritualities, for Carr spirituality is essentially religious and a secular spirituality would be 'tantamount to a contradiction in terms' (Carr, 1996a, p. 176). Certainly a spiritual virtue like holiness may properly be thought of as something more than a pattern of life, if it is seen as a spiritual orientation or character derived from a relation with God (Hebblethwaite, 1997, p. 51).

Charles Taylor, by contrast, offers a broader understanding of the spiritual as constituting a 'background picture' of strong evaluation that incorporates, but points beyond, the moral and personal. Spiritual concerns connect here with our ideals and our sense of what makes life meaningful and generally worth living.

> While it may not be judged a moral lapse that I am living a life that is not really worthwhile or fulfilling, to describe me in these terms is nevertheless to condemn me in the name of a standard, independent of my own tastes and desires, which I ought to acknowledge. (Taylor, 1989, p. 4)

These spiritual values are not public and agreed in the same way as are the values of 'morality in the narrow sense' (which consists of universally-recognised 'public virtues' and obligations to others). They form a part of 'ethics' when that term is used for our broad concerns about what comprises the good life, reserving 'morality' for the narrower area set within this (see above pp. 2 and 8).

Transcending values?

In identifying the nature of these spiritual values, perhaps we may speak in terms of transcending values or commitments.

In what ways do they 'go beyond'? First, they are our *deepest commitments*, operating at the most fundamental motivational level: richer, deeper and wider even than the morality to which they give rise (Evans, 1979). They lie beyond and beneath morality as its fundamental ground and – essentially religious – foundation (cf. Mavrodes, 1986, p. 226).

Second, spirituality constitutes a *transcending perspective* by which the true, mature self reaches out to what is beyond itself, by letting go of security and defensiveness in order to truly live and fully love. This is the life which we choose as we become ourselves by losing ourselves (Mark 8:35–37).

Crucified values

Look back to the list of values that you generated at the beginning of this chapter. What do we really value, if we are honest (Christians included): life, health and sex; security, shelter and happiness; work and love; friends and family; even success, status and power? Is Christianity the confirmation of *all* such valuing or does it involve the overturning of some of it?

Paul wrote to the Church in Corinth, 'I decided to know nothing among you except Jesus Christ, and him crucified.'

EXERCISE
📖 **Read 1 Corinthians 2 and 2 Corinthians 4:1–12.**

What is Paul's view of the distinction between worldly and Christian spirituality and wisdom?

Paul sees the wisdom of Christ as over against the wisdom of the world. The wisdom of Christ is a crucified wisdom, a wisdom of the cross. In value terms, it may be thought of as a crucifixion of some of our dearest and most closely held values, including the values of self and security, and especially the values of worldly status, authority and power (cf. John 19:8–11).

What is Christian living? It is certainly not concerned with becoming someone or being someone (even a saint), nor with building up one's character and moral status in a pride-ful or defensive manner. It is more about *kenosis* – emptying oneself of self, for others and for no reward. 'We must be good for nothing . . . good without reward or consolation' (Cupitt, 1986, p. 164).

The power displayed in the cross, to which the resurrection bears witness, is a power made perfect in weakness. This redefines the power of power and reveals secular authority for what (and all) it is. The centurion, the symbol of worldly power, sees the broken Christ and confesses that this man was truly of God (Mark 15:39). This is worship, 'worth-ship': the ascription of supreme worth, the recognition of true value. Religion is essentially about our proper worship.

From one viewpoint the cross is only defeat: the death of humility, integrity, honesty, compassion and love. Yet conversion to Christianity, understood essentially as a value or character conversion (cf. Lang, 1931, p. 189), allows Christians to see the cross as the victory of these values. This is not a worldly victory, however, not even of the sort that happened when non-violence empowered the Indian nation, but a *spiritual* one. It is a recognition of *another order of valuing*. Hence 'heavenly success is not another form of success' and spiritual greatness is 'not a species of greatness, but a greatness that lies outside the totality of ways of being great' (Moore, 1988, pp. 172, 179).

In the eyes of the world, the cross is failure. From the spiritual perspective, the theological perspective and the eternal perspective, it is the triumph of God. The cross is essentially a radical *re-vision*, a new onlook. 'When I survey the wondrous cross . . . my richest gains I count but loss, and pour contempt on all my pride.' The value conversion that Christianity offers is to *see through* the worldly values, as a preliminary to falling in love with and embracing the crucified values. To worship Christ is to ascribe supreme worth to the way and values of Jesus, the one who is crucified.

Talk of values is always talk about choosing sides. Holding a value is often a preliminary to becoming involved in a battle of values. So we ought to consider carefully the nature of our values – and which of them *we* might be willing to fight for and die for.

This is the sense in which Christianity may be described as an overturning of values and a crucifixion of the wisdom of this world. This is what is meant by 'choosing life' – through death.

Further reading

Introductory

Baelz, P (1977), *Ethics and Belief*, London, Sheldon.
Baelz, P (1996), Morality and religion, *Dialogue*, 6, 36–39.

Advanced

Bartley, W W (1971), *Morality and Religion*, London, Macmillan.
Gustafson, J M (1981), *Theology and Ethics*, Oxford, Blackwell.
Grenz, S J (1997), *The Moral Quest: foundations of Christian ethics*, Leicester, Apollos, chapters 7 and 8.
Moore, G (1988), *Believing in God: a philosophical essay*, Edinburgh, T and T Clark, chapter 5.
Mounce, H O (1998), Morality and religion, in B Davies (ed.), *Philosophy of Religion: a guide to the subject*, chapter 9, London, Cassell.
O'Donovan, O M T (1994), *Resurrection and Moral Order: an outline for evangelical ethics*, Leicester, Apollos.

REFERENCES

Advisory Council for the Church's Ministry (1974), *Teaching Christian Ethics: an approach*, London, SCM.

Almond, B (1994), New occasions teach new duties, *The Expository Times*, 105, 164–167.

Aquinas (1963–1975), *Summa Theologiae*, ET ed. T Gilby, London, Eyre and Spottiswoode (60 vols).

Argyle, M (1987), *The Psychology of Happiness*, London, Routledge.

Arrington, R L (1989), *Rationalism, Realism, and Relativism: perspectives in contemporary moral epistemology*, Ithaca, Cornell University Press.

Astley, J (1994), *The Philosophy of Christian Religious Education*, Birmingham, Alabama, Religious Education Press.

Astley, J (1998), Christian values and the management of schools, in W K Kay and L J Francis (eds), *Religion in Education: 2*, pp. 353–386, Leominster, Gracewing.

Astley, J (2000), *God's World*, London, Darton, Longman and Todd.

Baelz, P (1977), *Ethics and Belief*, London, Sheldon.

Baier, K (1973), Moral autonomy as an aim of moral education, in G Langford and D J O'Connor (eds), *New Essays in the Philosophy of Education*, chapter 6, London, Routledge.

Baron, M W (1997), Kantian ethics, in M W Baron, P Pettit and M Slote, *Three Methods of Ethics: a debate*, chapter 1, Oxford, Blackwell.

Barrett, C K (1971), *A Commentary on the First Epistle to the Corinthians*, London, A and C Black.

Barth, K (1961), *Church Dogmatics, Vol. III/IV, 4*, ET Edinburgh, T and T Clark.

Bellah, R N; Madsen, R; Sullivan, W M; Swidler, A; Tipton, S (1985), *Habits of the Heart: individualism and commitment in American life*, Berkeley, California, University of California Press.

Blackburn, S (1998), *Ruling Passions: a theory of practical reasoning*, Oxford, Clarendon.

Borg, M J and Wright, N T (1999), *The Meaning of Jesus: two visions*, London, SPCK.

Bowker, J (1994), Introduction: raising the issues, in J Holm and J Bowker (eds), *Making Moral Decisions*, pp. 1–16, London, Cassell.

Braine, J (1989), *Room at the Top*, London, Reed.

Braithwaite, R B (1955), *An Empiricist's View of the Nature of Religious Belief,* Cambridge, Cambridge University Press.

Brueggemann, W (1996), Passion and perspective: two dimensions of education in the Bible, in J Astley, L J Francis and C Crowder (eds), *Theological Perspectives on Christian Formation: a reader on theology and Christian education,* pp. 71–79, Leominster, Gracewing.

Brümmer, V (1981), *Theology and Philosophical Inquiry: an introduction,* London, Macmillan.

Brümmer, V (1993), *The Model of Love,* Cambridge, Cambridge University Press.

Burnaby, J (1967), Augustine of Hippo, in J Macquarrie (ed.), *A Dictionary of Christian Ethics,* pp. 22–24, London, SCM.

Butler, J (1726), *Fifteen Sermons,* various editions.

Caird, G B (1994), *New Testament Theology,* ed. L D Hurst, Oxford, Clarendon.

Carr, D (1991), *Educating the Virtues: an essay on the philosophical psychology of moral development in education,* London, Routledge.

Carr, D (1995), Towards a distinctive conception of spiritual education, *Oxford Review of Education,* 21, 83–98.

Carr, D (1996a), Rival conceptions of spiritual education, *Journal of Philosophy of Education,* 30, 2, 159–178.

Carr, D (1996b), *The Moral Role of the Teacher,* Edinburgh, Scottish Consultative Council on the Curriculum.

Christian Education Movement (1995), *What the Churches Say: on moral and social issues,* Derby, CEM.

Cook, D (1983), *The Moral Maze: a way of exploring Christian ethics,* London, SPCK.

Cupitt, D (1986), *Life Lines,* London, SCM.

Cupitt, D (1988), *The New Christian Ethics,* London, SCM.

Dancy, J (1993), An ethic of prima facie duties, in P Singer (ed.), *A Companion to Ethics,* chapter 18, Oxford, Blackwell.

David, M E (ed.) (1998), *The Fragmented Family: does it matter?* London, IEA Health and Welfare Unit.

Davies, J (1996), A preferential option for the family, in S C Barton (ed.), *The Family in Theological Perspective,* chapter 12, Edinburgh, T and T Clark.

Davies, J (ed.) (1993), *The Family: is it just another lifestyle choice?* London, IEA Health and Welfare Unit.

Deidun, T (1998), The Bible and Christian ethics, in B Hoose (ed.), *Christian Ethics: an introduction,* chapter 1, London, Cassell.

Dillenberger, J (ed.) (1961), *Martin Luther: selections from his writings,* Garden City, New York, Doubleday.

Dodd, C H (1951), *Gospel and Law,* Cambridge, Cambridge University Press.

Dower, N (1993), World poverty, in P Singer (ed.) (1993), *A Companion to Ethics,* chapter 23, Oxford, Blackwell.

Downie, R S (1971), *Roles and Values: an introduction to social ethics,* London, Methuen.

Downie, R S (1975), The justification of punishment, in J Rachels (ed.), *Moral*

Problems: a collection of philosophical essays, pp. 219–227, New York, Harper and Row.

Evans, D (1979), *Struggle and Fulfillment*, Cleveland, Collins.

Evans, D (1993), *Spirituality and Human Nature*, Albany, New York, State University of New York Press.

Evans, R (1999), *Using the Bible*, London, Darton, Longman and Todd.

Fletcher, J (1966), *Situation Ethics: the new morality*, London, SCM.

Francis, L J and Kay, W K (1995), *Teenage Religion and Values*, Leominster, Gracewing.

Frankena, W K (1973), *Ethics*, Englewood Cliffs, New Jersey, Prentice-Hall.

General Synod Marriage Commission (1978), *Marriage and the Church's Task*, London, Church Information Office.

Gensler, H J (1998), *Ethics: a contemporary introduction*, London, Routledge.

Gill, R (1999), *Churchgoing and Christian Ethics*, Cambridge, Cambridge University Press.

Gilligan, C (1982), *In a Different Voice: psychological theory and women's development*, Cambridge, Massachusetts, Harvard University Press.

Glover, J (1977), *Causing Death and Saving Lives*, Harmondsworth, Penguin.

Glover, J (1999), *Humanity: a moral history of the twentieth century*, London, Jonathan Cape.

Gorringe, T J (1998), Property, in B Hoose (ed.), *Christian Ethics: an introduction*, chapter 12, London, Cassell.

Grenz, S J (1997), *The Moral Quest: foundations of Christian ethics*, Leicester, Apollos.

Grimshaw, J (1993), The idea of a female ethic, in P Singer (ed.) (1993), *A Companion to Ethics*, chapter 43, Oxford, Blackwell.

Gustafson, J M (1981), *Theology and Ethics*, Oxford, Blackwell.

Halstead, M and Taylor, M J (eds) (1996), *Values in Education and Education in Values*, London, Falmer.

Hare, R M (1992), *Essays on Religion and Education*, Oxford, Clarendon.

Harvey, N P (1991), *The Morals of Jesus*, London, Darton, Longman and Todd.

Hauerwas, S (1980), Character, narrative, and growth in the Christian life, in J Fowler and A Vergote (eds), *Toward Moral and Religious Maturity*, pp. 441–484, Morriston, New Jersey, Silver Burdett.

Hauerwas, S (1981), *A Community of Character: toward a constructive Christian social ethic*, Notre Dame, Indiana, University of Notre Dame Press.

Hauerwas, S (1984), *The Peaceable Kingdom: a primer in Christian ethics*, London, SCM.

Haydon, G (1999), Values, virtues and violence: education and the public understanding of morality, *Journal of Philosophy of Education*, 33, 1, v –156.

Hays, R B (1996), *The Moral Vision of the New Testament: community, cross, new creation*, Edinburgh, T and T Clark.

Hebblethwaite, B (1997), *Ethics and Religion in a Pluralistic Age*, Edinburgh, T and T Clark.

Hick, J (1983), *The Second Christianity*, London, SCM.

Higginson, R (1997), *The Ethics of Business Competition: the law of the jungle?* Cambridge, Grove Books.

Hodgson, P C (1994), *Winds of the Spirit: a constructive Christian theology*, London, SCM.

Hoggart, R (1957), *The Uses of Literacy*, Harmondsworth, Penguin.

Holloway, R (1999), *Godless Morality: keeping religion out of ethics*, Edinburgh, Canongate.

Hospers, J (1972), *Human Conduct: problems of ethics*, New York, Harcourt Brace Jovanovich.

Josephus (1981), *The Jewish War*, ET Harmondsworth, Penguin.

Kant, I (1948), *The Moral Law: Kant's Groundwork of the Metaphysics of Morals*, ET London, Hutchinson.

Kant, I (1996), *The Metaphysics of Morals*, ET Cambridge, Cambridge University Press.

Keeling, M (1970), *Morals in a Free Society*, London, SCM.

Kohlberg, L (1981), *The Philosophy of Moral Development: moral stages and the idea of justice*, New York, Harper and Row.

Kohlberg, L; Levine, C; Hewer, A (1984), *Moral Stages: a current formulation and a response to critics*, Basel, Karger.

Küng, H and Schmidt, H (eds) (1998), *A Global Ethic and Global Responsibilities: two declarations*, London, SCM.

Lang, L W (1931), *A Study of Conversion: an enquiry into the development of Christian personality*, London, Allen and Unwin.

Lebacqz, K (1998), Social ethics, in B Hoose (ed.), *Christian Ethics: an introduction*, chapter 11, London, Cassell.

Lehmann, P L (1963), *Ethics in a Christian Context*, New York, Harper and Row.

Lewis, C S (1963), *The Four Loves*, London, Collins.

Locke, J (1698), *Two Treatises of Government*, various editions.

Lohmeyer, E (1965), *The Lord's Prayer*, ET London, Collins.

MacIntyre, A (1981), *After Virtue: a study in moral theory*, London, Duckworth.

Mackie, J L (1977), *Ethics: inventing right and wrong*, Harmondsworth, Penguin.

Mackinnon, D M (1957), *A Study in Ethical Theory*, London, A and C Black.

Marx, K (1875), *Critique of the Gotha Programme*, various editions.

Mavrodes, G I (1986), Religion and the queerness of morality, in R Audi and W J Wainwright (eds), *Rationality, Religious Belief and Moral Commitment*, chapter 8, Ithaca, New York, Cornell University Press.

McLaughlin, T H (1995), Liberalism, education and the common school, *Journal of Philosophy of Education*, 29, 2, 239–255.

Midgley, M (1991), *Can't We Make Moral Judgements?*, Bristol, Bristol Press.

Mill, J S (1962), *Utilitarianism, On Liberty, Essays on Bentham*, ed. M Warnock, London, Collins.

Moore, G (1988), *Believing in God: a philosophical essay*, Edinburgh, T and T Clark.

Moore, G (1998), Sex, sexuality and relationships, in B Hoose (ed.), *Christian Ethics: an introduction*, chapter 16, London, Cassell.

Morgan, P (1999), *Farewell to the Family? Public policy and family breakdown in Britain and the USA*, London, IEA Health and Welfare Unit.

Murdoch, I (1992), *Metaphysics as a Guide to Morals*, London, Chatto and Windus.

Niebuhr, R (1932), *Moral Man and Immoral Society: a study in ethics and politics*, New York, Scribner's.

Nineham, D (1976), *The Use and Abuse of the Bible: a study of the Bible in an age of rapid cultural change*, London, SPCK.

Nowell-Smith, P (1999), Morality: religious and secular, in E Stump and M J Murray (eds), *Philosophy of Religion: the big questions*, chapter 45, Oxford, Blackwell.

Nozick, R (1974), *Anarchy, State and Utopia*, Oxford, Blackwell.

Nygren, A (1932), *Agapé and Eros*, ET London, SPCK.

Oppenheimer, H (1962), *Law and Love*, London, Faith Press.

Pence, G (1993), Virtue theory, in P Singer (ed.), *A Companion to Ethics*, chapter 21, Oxford, Blackwell.

Pettit, P (1997), The consequentialist perspective, in M W Baron, P Pettit and M Slote, *Three Methods of Ethics: a debate*, chapter 2, Oxford, Blackwell.

Piaget, J (1932), *The Moral Judgement of the Child*, London, Routledge and Kegan Paul.

Potter, H (1993), *Hanging in Judgement: religion and the death penalty in England from the Bloody Code to abolition*, London, SCM.

Preston, R (1993), Christian ethics, in P Singer (ed.), *A Companion to Ethics*, chapter 8, Oxford, Blackwell.

Price, H H (1969), *Belief*, London, George, Allen and Unwin.

Pring, R (1996), Markets, education and Catholic schools, in T H McLaughlin, J O'Keefe and B O'Keeffe (eds), *The Contemporary Catholic School: context, identity and diversity*, pp. 57–69, London, Falmer.

Rachels, J (1999), *The Elements of Moral Philosophy*, Singapore, McGraw-Hill.

Ramsey, P (1953), *Basic Christian Ethics*, London, SCM.

Ramsey, P (1967), *Deeds and Rules in Christian Ethics*, New York, Scribner's.

Rawls, J (1972), *A Theory of Justice*, Oxford, Oxford University Press.

Reeves, M and Kaye, E (1999), Tracts for wartime: *The Christian News-Letter*, in M Reeves (ed.), *Christian Thinking and Social Order: conviction politics from the 1930s to the present day*, chapter 3, London, Cassell.

Robb, B (1996), Values education as a better way to develop responsible behaviour: some implications for philosophy of education, *Philosophy of Education Society of Great Britain Newsletter*, 23–24.

Robb, W M (1994), *Values Education: can it alleviate social problems?*, Aberdeen, CAVE.

Ross, W D (1930), *The Right and The Good*, Oxford, Clarendon.

Rousseau, J-J (1754), *A Discussion on the Origin of Inequality*, various editions.

Royal Commission on Capital Punishment (1953), *Report*, London, HMSO.

Schweitzer, A (1954), *The Quest of the Historical Jesus: a critical study of its progress from Reimarus to Wrede*, ET London, A and C Black.

Schweitzer, A (1968), *The Kingdom of God and Primitive Christianity*, ET London, A and C Black.

Scruton, R (1998), *An Intelligent Person's Guide to Modern Culture*, London, Duckworth.

Sidgwick, H (1907), *The Methods of Ethics*, London, Macmillan.

Slote, M (1997), Virtue ethics, in M W Baron, P Pettit and M Slote, *Three Methods of Ethics*, chapter 3, Oxford, Blackwell.

Smart, J J C (1973), An outline of a system of utilitarian ethics, in J J C Smart and B Williams, *Utilitarianism For and Against*, pp. 3–74, Cambridge, Cambridge University Press.

Solomon, R C (1993), Business ethics, in P Singer (ed.), *A Companion to Ethics*, chapter 31, Oxford, Blackwell.

Spohn, W C (1999), *Go and Do Likewise: Jesus and ethics*, New York, Continuum.

Sprigge, T L S (1988), *The Rational Foundations of Ethics*, London, Routledge and Kegan Paul.

Strange, W (2000), *The Authority of the Bible*, London, Darton, Longman and Todd.

Taylor, C (1989), *Sources of the Self*, Cambridge, Cambridge University Press.

Ten, C L (1993), Crime and punishment, in P Singer (ed.), *A Companion to Ethics*, chapter 32, Oxford, Blackwell.

Thiessen, E J (1993), *Teaching for Commitment: liberal education, indoctrination and religious nurture*, Leominster, Gracewing.

Thomson, J J (1975), A defense of abortion, in J Rachels (ed.), *Moral Problems: a collection of philosophical essays*, pp. 89–106, New York, Harper and Row.

Towler, R (1984), *The Need for Certainty: a sociological study of conventional religion*, London, Routledge and Kegan Paul.

Vardy, P (1992), *The Puzzle of Evil*, London, HarperCollins.

Wakefield, G S (1983), Spirituality, in A Richardson and J Bowden (eds), *A New Dictionary of Christian Theology*, pp. 549–550, London, SCM.

Ward, K (1970), *Ethics and Christianity*, George, Allen and Unwin.

Ward, K (1976), *The Divine Image: the foundations of Christian morality*, London, SCM.

Warnock, M (1996), Moral values, in M Halstead and M J Taylor (eds), *Values in Education and Education in Values*, pp. 45–53, London, Falmer.

Warnock, M (1998), *An Intelligent Person's Guide to Ethics*, London, Duckworth.

Wasserstrom, R (1975a), Rights, human rights, and racial discrimination, in J Rachels (ed.), *Moral Problems: a collection of philosophical essays*, pp. 109–122, New York, Harper and Row.

Wasserstrom, R (1975b), On the morality of war: a preliminary inquiry, in J Rachels (ed.), *Moral Problems: a collection of philosophical essays*, pp. 298–331, New York, Harper and Row.

White, V (1991), *Atonement and Incarnation: an essay in universalism and particularity*, Cambridge, Cambridge University Press.

White, V (1996), *Paying Attention to People: an essay on individualism and Christian belief*, London, SPCK.

Wong, D (1993), Relativism, in P Singer (ed.), *A Companion to Ethics*, chapter 39, Oxford, Blackwell.

Wood, T (1961), *Some Moral Problems*, London, SPCK.

GLOSSARY AND BIOGRAPHY

agnostic not knowing (particularly whether God exists)

allegory a story in which the meaning or message is represented symbolically

Aquinas, St Thomas (1225–1274) philosopher and theologian

Aristotle (384–322 BC) Greek philosopher

Augustine, St (354–430) theologian and Bishop of Hippo in North Africa

autonomy the state of being independent and 'self-governed' (as opposed to **heteronomy**)

Barth, Karl (1886–1968) Swiss Protestant theologian

Bell, George K A (1881–1958) Anglican Bishop of Chichester

Calvin, John (1509–1564) French Protestant Reformer

Camara, Helder (1909–1999) Catholic Archbishop in Brazil

Chrysostom, St John (c. 347–407) theologian and Bishop of Constantinople

Cicero, Marcus Tullius (106–43 BC) Roman orator and statesman

communitarians those who claim that a society, with its ties of affection, kinship and common purpose, is more than the individuals within it and their contractual obligations

conscience our consciousness of what is right and wrong

consequentialism/teleology an approach to ethics that holds that the rightness of an action depends on its promoting good consequences

cultural relativity the factual claim that different societies think differently

deontology/nonconsequentialism an approach to ethics that holds that certain sorts of acts are right or wrong in themselves, quite apart from their consequences

divine command theory the view that the right and the good are determined by God's will

egoism the view that we ought to do what maximises self-interest (**ethical egoism**) or that we are always in fact so motivated (**psychological egoism**)

emotivism the view that moral claims are expressions of emotions

Enlightenment, the eighteenth-century 'Age of Reason', advocated 'trusting your own reason' and critical of reliance on authority and tradition

eschatology beliefs about 'the end of history', 'the future hope' and the 'last things' (death, judgement, heaven and hell)

eternity state of everlasting or timeless existence

expressivism/subjectivism the view that moral judgements are based on, and express or prescribe, human subjective states

Freud, Sigmund (1856–1939) Austrian psychiatrist, originator of psychoanalysis

fundamentalism the view that the Bible contains no errors

Gandhi, Mahatma (1869–1948) Indian statesman

hermeneutics the art or science of interpretation

Hobbes, Thomas (1588–1679) English philosopher

Hume, David (1711–1776) Scottish Enlightenment philosopher

immutable unchanging

Josephus, Flavius (c. 37– c. 100) Jewish historian

justice treating others as they have a right to be treated: whether 'equally' or 'fairly' **(distributive justice)** or to rectify an injustice **(retributive justice)**

Kant, Immanuel (1724–1804) German Enlightenment philosopher

kenosis the 'self-emptying' or renunciation of the divine nature, at least in part, by Christ at his incarnation ('enfleshing')

liberation theology a type of theology that stresses justice and freedom from dependence, particularly for the poor

Locke, John (1632–1704) English philosopher

Luther, Martin (1483–1546) German Protestant Reformer

maxim a principle on which people act

middle axioms provisional maxims of behaviour, or realisable moral objectives, intermediate between universal principles and specific situations

moral realism the view that moral judgements are grounded in the nature of things and are objectively right or wrong, independently of subjective and variable human reactions

moral relativism the view that moral truths are not universal but relative to the standpoint of those who make moral judgements

natural law theory the view that moral principles may be discovered by a rational study of human nature

Niebuhr, Reinhold (1892–1971) American practical theologian

Ockham, William (1285–1347) English Franciscan philosopher

original sin the inherited, defective state of human beings since the Fall, in which our freedom to do good is destroyed or limited

Paine, Thomas (1737–1809) English political theorist

Paley, William (1743–1805) Anglican theologian and apologist

Plato (c. 429–347 BC) Greek philosopher

postmodernism philosophical or cultural perspective that distrusts large-scale justifications of truth and celebrates extreme relativism

prescriptive having the quality of an imperative (command)

Ramsey, Arthur Michael (1904–1988) Anglican theologian and Archbishop of Canterbury

rights, human liberties that we may exercise, or claims that we can justifiably demand of others, simply because we are human beings

Rousseau, John-Jacques (1712–1778) French philosopher and novelist

Ruskin, John (1819–1900) English art and social critic

sanctification the process of 'being made holy' by God's transforming grace, often through a gradual growth in the Christian life

Schweitzer, Albert (1875–1965) German theologian, organist and medical missionary

situation ethics the view that every situation must be judged on its merits and not in terms of common features or rules

speech-act an act performed by an utterance (stating, expressing, promising, frightening etc.)

transcendence state of excelling or surpassing; being beyond and above experience, language, knowledge and thought

universalisability feature of moral judgements that they should apply in other identical cases

utilitarianism the view that we ought to perform the act that produces the best consequences for everyone (**act-utilitarianism**) or to follow those rules that yield the best consequences when everyone follows them (**rule-utilitarianism**)

virtue, moral morally admirable character trait, disposing us to right action

Vitoria, Francisco de (c. 1485–1546) Spanish Dominican philosopher and theologian

voluntarism a viewpoint that emphasises the will

Von Hügel, Friedrich (1852–1925) Roman Catholic lay theologian

INDEX OF THEMES

abortion 38–44
absolute morality 87, 90, 95, 101
adultery 54
agape 30
altruism 30, 96
annulment 53
atheists 112
attitudes 92–94, 102–103
autonomy of agents 57–59, 71, 87, 100, 106–107
autonomy of ethics 109, 111–112

beliefs, religious 113
Bible and ethics 25–33, 36, 43, 47, 52, 54, 65, 67, 75, 82, 83, 84, 100, 106, 112, 114
blame 3, 89
body 51
business ethics 69–71

cannibalism 92
care, ethic of 57–59, cf. 69
casuistry 35
categorical imperative 4, 20, 22, 89–90
Catholic ethics 33–35, 44, 47, 53
celibacy 51–52, 55
character *see* virtue
Christian ethics ix, 9, 10, 18, 24–37, 43–44, 53–56, 66–71, 77–79, 83–85, 106, 109–118
commitment, moral 102, 116
communism 66–67

communitarians 9, 65
community, moral 69, 99, 103, 104, 105 *see also* communitarians
concupiscence 51
conscience 34, 87, 112
consequences 12, 14, 15, 18, 19, 36 *see also* utilitarianism
contraception 35, 52, 55–56
conversion, moral 25, 106–107, 117
creation 29, 51, 61
criticism, moral/critical moral education 91–92, 101, 102, 106–107
crucifixion 78–79, 116–118

death 113
decision-making 1, 10, 35–36, 57–59, 86, 101
deontological ethics 18–22, 33–35, 80
deterrence 77, 80–81
development, moral 56–57, 98–99
Didache 43
disagreement in ethics 86–97
discrimination 66, 77
disinterestedness 32–33
disposition, moral 105
divine command theory 33, 110–111, 113
divorce 52–54
double effect 6–7, 22, 44, 45, 76
duties, prima facie 21
duty 7, 19, 23, 57, 59, 96, 111 *see also* deontological ethics

education, character 99, 100
education, moral 86, 88, 98–107
education, values 99–101
egoism, ethical 12–13
egoism, psychological 13–14
emotivism 93
ends of life 7–8, 34–35, 111, 115–116
equality 64, 65–66, 94, 96
ethics and morality 2, 8, 116
euthanasia 35, 38, 44–47
Euthyphro dilemma 110–113
exemplars, moral 9, 106, 110
expressivism 93, 101, 102

Fall 34, 51, 61
families 53–55, 59, 104
feelings 92–94, 103
female ethic 56–59
flourishing 8, 111
forgiveness 84–85, 96
formation, moral 99, 101–107
formalism 19–20
freedom 64, 101

gender 56
gift of life, the 47
golden rule 18, 29–30, 41, 65, 94, 104
good life, the 7–10, 58–59, 111
good/bad 1–2, 7–10
grace 28, 29, 114

happiness/pleasure 7, 15, 50, 52, 56
holiness 115
homosexuality 54–55

ideal spectator 93
imitation of Christ 31–32, 110
impartiality 5, 9, 17, 20, 30, 59, 65
indoctrination 106
integrity 3
intention 6–7, 22, 45, 99
interim ethic 28
intuition, moral 36, 90

Jesus 27–32, 52, 67, 75, 78–79, 84, 116–118
Jewish ethics 51–52, 61
judging people 88–89
just war theory 76–77
justice, commutative 64
justice, distributive 16, 20, 21, 62–66, 94, 96
justice, ethic of 57, 62–63, 70, 77–78
justice, retributive 80, 83

Kantian ethics 4, 19–20, 22, 80, 83, 89–90, 111
kenosis 117

language/grammar of morality 1–5, 92, 101, 102
liberal democrats 66
liberals 65, 100
liberty 96
love 18, 23, 30–31, 94, 96, 113

market economy 66–68, 69–71
market liberals 66
marriage 36, 52–54
maxims 20
means and ends 16, 20, 32–33, 69, 81, 83, 89–90, 96
middle axioms 35
modelling 102, 103, 106
moral philosophy 2
morally identical situations 4–5
motive 8, 10, 22–23, 32, 36, 81, 114, 116
murder 18, 22, 74, 83, 94

natural law 34–35, 47, 55, 56, 111–112
neighbours 30, 86–97, 114
neutrality 100
non-violence 77–79, 94, 117
norms *see* rules
nuclear war/deterrence 77

objective morality 90, 92, 101, 105

obligation 7, 10, 17, 95, 104 *see also* duty

ought 4, 35

overridingness 87–88

pacifism 74–76, 77–79

pay 62–64

person, concept of 40, 69

phenomenology, moral 91, 101

pluralism, moral 33, 86–97

political realism 74, 76

postmodernism 91–92

poverty 66, 68–69

power 117

pre-marital sex 49–50, 54

prescription 93, 94, 102

principles 9, 19–20, 35, 57, 94, 99, 102, 107

privatisation of morality 87

promises 16, 17, 20, 36

property 67–68

proportionality 77, 83

protection 82

Protestant/Anglican ethics 33, 47, 53, 54, 65, 82

prudence 28, 74

punishment 79–85, 86

punishment, capital 82–83

realism, moral 90

reason/rationality 20, 33, 41, 57, 90, 92, 93, 98–99, 101, 104–105, 107, 112 *see also* natural law

reciprocity 28–29

reform 81

relationships 57–59, 84–85

relativism, moral 90–92, 101

relativity, cultural 90

religion and morality 109–118 *see also* Christian ethics

respect 89–90, 102

response, ethic of 84, 113–115

responsibility 6–7, 89–90, 96, 100

retaliation 77, 78, cf. 80

retribution 80, 83–84

revelation 33, 34, 90

rewards 32–33, 62–63, 117

right to life 40, 42–43, 46, 74–76

right/wrong 1–5, 7, 95, 99

rights 9, 39–40, 42–43, 64, 75, 77, 95–97

rules 16–17, 19–20, 34–36, 99, 102

sanctification 112

sanctity of life 40, 44, 47, 74–75, 82, 113

self-realisation 7, 96, 111, 115–116

sex/sexuality 49–59, 94

sin 49, 109

situation ethics 36, 57

social contract theory 20, 65

spirituality 112, 113, 115–118

status 117

stories 9, 106

subjectivism, moral 90, 92–94, 101

suicide 45, 47

supererogation 17

teleological ethics 19 *see also* utilitarianism

tolerance 87–89, 94

Trinity, the 113

truth 78, 94

truth, moral 90, 94, 101

universal morality 90–91, 94–96

universalisability 4–5, 17, 20, 57, 87, 93, 101 *see also* relativism, rights

utilitarianism 14–18, 39, 46, 63, 80–83

utilitarianism, act- 16–17, 36

utilitarianism, rule- 17, 36

values 7–8, 35, 99–100, 101, 105, 109, 110, 112, 115–118

values, crucified 116–118

values, transcending 116

vindication 79

virtue ethics 8–10, 22–23, 30–31, 59, 70, 84, 88, 100, 102–104, 115–118

vision, moral 105, 117 *see also* intuition, moral

war 73–79
wealth 61–71

wealth, redistribution of 64–65, 66,
  68–69
wisdom 116–118
work 61–63
worship 117

Applying for the Church Colleges'
Certificate Programme

The certificate programme is available in Anglican Church Colleges of Higher Education throughout England and Wales. There are currently hundreds of students on this programme, many with no previous experience of study of this kind. There are no entry requirements. Some people choose to take Certificate courses for their own interest and personal growth, others take these courses as part of their training for ministry in the church. Some go on to complete the optional assignments and, after the successful completion of three courses, gain the Certificate. Courses available through the *Exploring Faith: theology for life* series are ideal for establishing ability and potential for studying theology and biblical studies at degree level, and they provide credit onto degree programmes.

For further details of the Church Colleges' Certificate programme, related to this series, please contact the person responsible for Adult Education in your local diocese or one of the colleges at the addresses provided:

The Administrator of Part-time Programmes, Department of Theology and Religious Studies, Chester College, Parkgate Road, CHESTER, CH1 4BJ ☎ 01244 375444

The Registry, Roehampton Institute, Froebel College, Roehampton Lane, LONDON, SW15 5PJ ☎ 020 8392 3087

The Registry, Canterbury Christ Church University College, North Holmes Road, CANTERBURY, CT1 1QU ☎ 01227 767700

The Registry, College of St Mark and St John, Derriford Road, PLY-MOUTH, PL6 8BH ☎ 01752 636892

The Registry, Trinity College, CARMARTHEN, Carmarthenshire, SA31 3EP ☎ 01267 676767

Church Colleges' Programme, The Registry, King Alfred's College, Sparkford Road, WINCHESTER, SO22 4NR ☎ 01962 841515

Part-time Programmes, The Registry, College of St Martin, Bowerham Road, LANCASTER, LA1 3JD ☎ 01524 384529